spirit of the
ELEPHANT
majestic giant of the animal kingdom

First published in 2008
Parragon
Queen Street House
4 Queen Street
Bath BA1 1HE, UK

Designed, produced, and packaged by Stonecastle Graphics Limited

Text by Gill Davies
Designed by Sue Pressley and Paul Turner
Edited by Philip de Ste. Croix
Picture research by Karen James

ISBN 978-1-4075-2511-2

Printed in China

spirit of the
ELEPHANT

majestic giant of the animal kingdom

Gill Davies

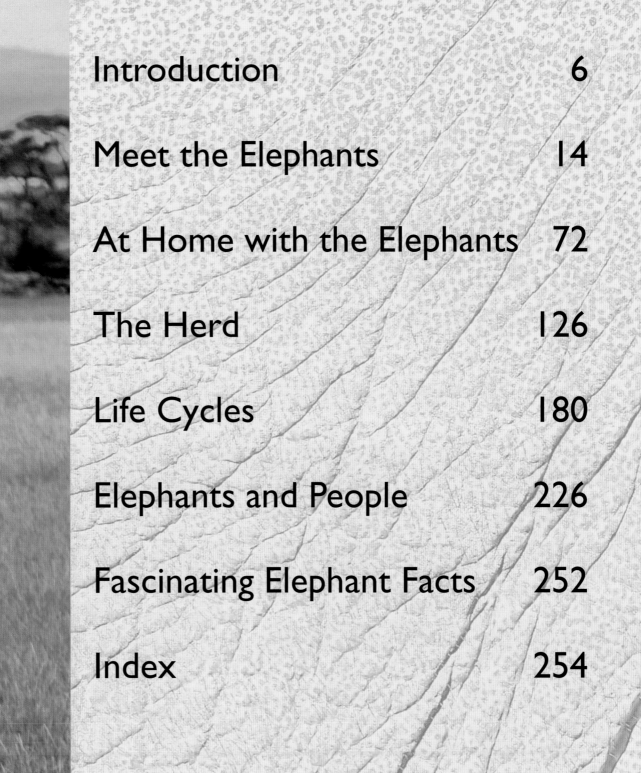

Contents

Introduction

The elephant is a **magnificent** creature, from the tip of its wrinkled **trunk** to the **tassel** at the end of its **tail**. It is immense, regal, and **awe-inspiring**. It is wise and **intelligent** and enjoys strong family bonds. In the **long grasses** of the African **savannah** and among the trees of the Asian **forests** we can learn more about the **elephant's life** and future.

Spirit of the Elephant

BASED ON a folk tale that probably originated in India, a poem by John Godfrey Saxe (1816-1887) called *The Blind Men and the Elephant* relates how six blind men each conjure up a mental picture of the elephant as they each feel a different part of its anatomy. One feels its side, one the tusk, one the trunk, one the leg, one the ear and finally, one the tail. In turn, each assumes the elephant is like a wall, a spear, a snake, a tree, a fan, and a rope:

> And so these men of Indostan
> Disputed loud and long,
> Each in his own opinion
> Exceeding stiff and strong,
> Though each was partly in the right,
> And all were in the wrong!

This is not altogether humorous nonsense for, even when able to view the elephant as a whole, each of us will have an individual perception of it, founded on our particular knowledge and experience of these impressive creatures. Some of us may even have been fortunate enough to have visited them in their domain. This is a privilege that I never fail to appreciate – and I remember it vividly as the highlight of an all-too-brief visit to Kenya. There, after days when elephants seemed just to flirt with us, appearing only as mere specks against the distant horizon, on our very last day in the Masai Mara, we suddenly found ourselves right next to a herd. They were busy munching away at trees, with a young baby cavorting in their midst. A mock charge by the youngster's mother soon put us in our place before they marched off, leaving us open-mouthed and stunned by the privilege of having spent just a few moments in their awe-inspiring presence.

Above: An African elephant. Unlike human teeth, elephant tusks are covered with a layer of cementum (calcified tissue) rather than an enamel coating. Up to one half of the tusk is hollow.

Opposite: A group of Asian elephants set off for a refreshing drink and perhaps a cooling splash, but first the youngsters greet each other by entwining trunks.

Previous pages: An elephant's wrinkled hide is thick on its back and sides but remains sensitive to the sun – so cooling off in water or a mudbath is vital to their well-being.

These amazing creatures are special in so many ways – from their appeal as small, shy, newborn babies to their gigantic size as mighty adults. They are strong enough to uproot trees with their trunks, but this part of their body can also manipulate things so delicately that it can pick up a feather. Elephants can exhibit a fierce temper during mating *musth* but also display gentle parental care. We cannot help but be impressed by their intelligence and memory, appreciate their joy when they frolic in water, be surprised by their prowess as swimmers, and by their ability to communicate over considerable distances. The elephant can inspire in us a wide range of emotions, many of which it also appears to feel.

This book discovers the lifestyle of African, Asian, and forest elephants. It looks at their ancestors – the hairy mammoths and mastodons – as well as present-day relatives such as manatees, dugongs, and hyraxes. It reveals their social life and family groups, looking at their complex behavior, how they find food and water, and how they raise their youngsters. It follows their lives through jungle and savannah in a precious habitat that is diminishing by the minute.

Some elephants live up in the mountains too, in places like Kilimanjaro, Mount Kenya, and the Himalayas. A number track their way through the hot Namibia desert, digging in the sand for water, while in Mali, where the

Sahara's sand dunes merge with scattered trees and shrubs, the elephants must trudge some 35 miles (56km) a day in pursuit of water. Their amazing determination is just one example of the elephant's remarkable adaptability.

During this exploration of both their relationship with each other and with mankind through the ages, many amazing facts emerge. Fresh discoveries about the elephant's intelligence and behavior seem to add to our knowledge almost daily.

If the art of communication reflects intelligence, then elephants score high. They are very 'talkative' – altering the size of their nostrils as air passes through the trunk in order to growl, snort, roar, bark, grumble, cry and emit low-frequency infrasound rumblings (some of which they detect at a distance through their feet) as well as a wide variety of trumpeting calls. Like many other animals, they occasionally seem to exhibit powers of telepathy but this, in fact, is probably due to their infrasonic hearing alerting them to something of which we are not aware.

Part of their appeal to us diminutive onlookers is because these giants seem to share some of our human characteristics – a similar lifespan and rate of development, close family relationships, a renowned memory, their warm reaction to birth and their display of grief at death. Sometimes they will pause and seem to reflect on their loss at the place where a relative has died in the past, even when no bones or physical signs of its presence remain. Elephants display strong loyalties and develop friendships that can last a lifetime.

Lead by a wise matriarch, most herds live in the savannah or the forest – where their presence contributes to the ecological balance. These powerful bulldozers drive passages through the trees and their droppings recycle trace elements and nutrients from the broken timber they have chewed. The debris of branches they leave in their wake shields new young grasses and shrubs from the feet and muzzles of browsers; thus elephants alter the landscape, felling trees but also encouraging the growth of saplings and natural regeneration in a constant cycle of clearance and new growth. It is estimated that around a third of tree species in West Africa rely on elephants to help their seeds germinate by passing through their digestive tracts.

Often their trails trace the most practical route through tangled shrub and they may eventually become the foundation for human pathways. These trails lead to pools (that the elephants have also created) and act as conduits that help the passage of rainwater to these waterholes – pools that increase in size as the elephants bathe and plaster their great torsos with copious amounts of glutinous mud. Meanwhile, their great weight and dabbling feet – as they delight in the opportunity to cool off in the water – help to create a seal on the pool bottom that helps to contain the water more effectively. Sometimes, tunneling with their trunks, elephants may also unlock other water supplies, hidden deep below apparently dry river beds. All the other thirsty animals in the vicinity benefit from these vital water sources – created and then maintained by elephant behavior.

In some cultures, elephants are endowed with regal status or are worshipped as gods. Sometimes they serve as auspicious mounts for kings and princes, while in folk tales and myths, countless anecdotes and fascinating stories can be found about them. It is said that a very small animal like a bird, mouse, or mongoose can terrify this giant and that elephants are so fearful of chameleons that they will beat a hasty retreat if one pops into view – but factual confirmation of this story remains elusive.

A special affection for the elephant may be established in our early childhood through a favorite toy or book, and reinforced by memorable television footage as we grow older. Worthy studies by skillful teams of dedicated

researchers and cameramen have created many fine programes and books that have added greatly to our knowledge of elephant behavior.

Today poaching and a vanishing habitat combine to take a heavy toll on elephant numbers. Many fear for the future of these magnificent beasts. It is hard to imagine the planet devoid of their stately presence. What would the world be like without elephant silhouettes etched black against a crimson sunset, or painting a parade of deep shadows on the dusty ground? We need to see their mighty torsos reflected in a limpid pool, appearing above rippling waves of golden grass, threading their way through dense foliage, splashing in water like laughing, frolicking children. We

Above: The silhouette of an elephant which is backlit by the early morning glow as the Sun rises on a new savannah day.

need to tremble in the presence of a solitary male standing poised to charge, ears and trunk alert to every signal – and to be seduced by the antics of a baby, weaving its way between the adults' legs to peep out at this all-too-enormous world, unaware of the fragility of its future.

We must strive to ensure that the 'wall, spear, snake, tree, fan, and rope,' which together make up the magnificent creature that is the elephant, may continue to impress, terrify, thrill, and enchant our children and grandchildren – and all the generations yet to come.

Meet the Elephants

The elephants that now **populate** the Earth are **descended** from prehistoric **mammoths** that once ranged over most of the globe. Today, **elephants** live in the **grasslands** and forests of Africa, India, and South-East Asia. While not as **hairy** as the mammoth, their **size** remains impressive as they **march** along, eating copiously, taking an occasional swim and **communicating** with great **affection** and **intelligence**.

What is an Elephant?

THE LARGEST mammal in the world is the whale but, so far as land animals are concerned, it is the elephant that wins the prize for size and weight. These are mammals on the grandest scale and they are also among the most intelligent on the planet – with an incredible social infrastructure and abilities that we have only recently, as a result of closer study, begun to appreciate.

Once upon a prehistoric time, their extinct relatives ranged just about everywhere across the globe except for Antarctica and Australia. Today, most elephants live in the grasslands of Africa and the forests of Asia but despite this reduced range, they remain a highly successful and remarkable species.

Right: A group of African elephants pause in the sunset. They need a constant supply of food to fuel their daily needs and spend at least 18 hours a day eating and traveling many miles to find sufficient quantities of food to sustain them.

Following pages: An elephant eats some 227kg (500lb) of leaves, grass, fruits, buds, branches, roots, and bark daily – while newborn babies suckle over 21 pints (10 liters) of milk.

Getting the order right

In the scientific classification of living things, the order containing elephants is called *Proboscidea* – its name deriving, appropriately, from the term proboscis, which means a long, flexible snout or trunk. Today, there are two major species in the elephant family – the African elephant *(Loxodonta africana)* and the Asian *(Elephas maximus)*.

In addition, there are several subspecies within these groups – the Sri Lankan elephant *(Elephas maximus maximus)*, the Indian elephant *(Elephas maximus indicus)*, and the Sumatran elephant *(Elephas maximus sumatranus)*. As recently as 2003, a further subspecies was identified as the Borneo pygmy elephant *(Elephas maximus borneensis)*.

Now, to add to the menu, the forest elephants of Africa *(Loxodonta cyclotis)*, have been classified by some experts as a distinct species from the African savannah elephant *(Loxodonta africana)* – a separation supported by DNA analysis but not finally agreed by all the powers that be that adjudicate in such matters.

The African elephant is found in 37 countries in many parts of sub-Saharan Africa. Small numbers of forest elephants live in the dense equatorial forests of west and central Africa with many of them being found in the Democratic Republic of Congo. Savannah elephants are far more widespread and trample their way through drier woodlands and grasslands and are most commonly seen in Kenya, Tanzania, Botswana, Zimbabwe, Namibia, and South Africa.

Scientists estimate today's world population of Asian elephants to be approximately 40,000, less than one tenth of the number of African elephants. These smaller-eared heavyweights prefer forested areas and transitional zones between forests and grasslands, wherever there is proximity to water, and ample and varied sources of food. They inhabit India, Sri Lanka, Myanmar (Burma), Indonesia, Thailand, Cambodia, Vietnam, Laos, Malaysia, Nepal, Bangladesh, and southern China.

Left and opposite: An African savannah elephant (left) is larger than its Asian counterpart (opposite) and has much bigger ears. The tips of their trunks are differently shaped too. There are far fewer Asian elephants than there are Africans.

Previous pages: The rather hairier African forest elephant (left) has only recently been classified as a distinct species. It usually lives deep in the forests, as do the Asian elephants (right).

Right: The rock hyrax, or dassie, that clucks, whistles, and squeals among cliffs, rocks, and trees in Africa and the Middle East is a rodent but, amazingly, it is very closely related to elephants. It has similar foot bones and long incisors.

Below: An elephant's close relative, the dugong, is warm-blooded, breathes air and suckles its young. It sometimes rises above the sea surface and so may have engendered myths about mermaids.

Above: Modern genetic testing has established that manatees are probably more closely related to elephants than any other living animal and may originally have evolved from land mammals.

Ancient ancestors and modern relatives

Sometime about 50 to 60 million years ago, the ancestors of the modern elephant (then only the size of a domestic pig) lived in a far wider range of environments than do today's elephants: they inhabited many different types of terrain from tropical rainforests to deserts, and from coastal zones to high altitudes. Few places did not resound to the beat of their footfalls but, as time passed, only the direct ancestors of the African, Asian, and forest elephants survived a succession of extreme environmental conditions that caused many less hardy species to go extinct.

Although, at a glance, they do not obviously resemble their larger cousins – and live in entirely different habitats – manatees, dugongs, and hyraxes (all belonging to the related group of animals known as *Paenungulata*) are the closest living relatives of today's elephants. Particularly appealing relatives are the rock hyraxes or dassies (in the *Hyracoidea* order) that scramble around African and Middle Eastern cliffs, rocks, and trees – looking more like giant guinea pigs than elephants. It is amazing to learn that in ancestral terms, these rather endearing-looking rodents are relatives of the huge elephants peacefully grazing on the plains.

Very recently, scientists at the University of Michigan in the United States discovered what they believe may be a missing link between ancient and modern elephants: a 27-million-year-old fossil belonging to a pig-sized tusked creature. It has been suggested that both mastodons and elephants originated in Africa but whatever is eventually decided, it seems that mastodons and elephants may well

have emerged five million years earlier than has previously been assumed.

At any rate, about 60 million years ago, hoofed animals evolved from large primitive mammal herbivores. Their evolution followed five lines of descent, of which one vanished along the way, to emerge as four groups today – whales and dolphins; horses, tapirs, and rhinos; cloven-hoofed or even-toed ungulates; and elephants. (While whales and dolphins may seen unlikely members of this group, scientific discoveries suggest that they are related to the even-toed ungulates, eventually returning to the sea to live.)

The African elephant was the only elephant to remain in this original domain and it evolved to become the savannah and forest elephants that still range there today. The common ancestor of both mammoths and Asian elephants split from the line of African elephants some six to seven million years ago. Then Asian elephants and mammoths diverged about half a million years later and the Asian elephant, although not nearly as woolly as mammoths, is distinctly hairier than its distant African relatives.

Above: This young (and rather hairy) relative of the mastodon lives at Pinnawela Elephant Orphanage in Sri Lanka.

Following pages: An adult Asian elephant crops plants in the jungle.

Mammoth and mastodon

Fossil evidence of the presence of mammoths and mastodons has been found all around the world. Mammoths were part of the elephant order (*Proboscidea*) and became extinct only relatively recently – in geological terms – about five thousand years ago. The mastodon (*Mammut americanum*) inhabited North America during the Ice Age (some penetrated into South America too) but seems to have preferred to live in forests, while mammoths were more at home in open grassland. The mastodon roamed North America from at least 3.75 million to around 11,000 years ago when they became extinct. They resembled

(but were distinct from) mammoths with blunter, conical-shaped teeth and straighter, more horizontal tusks.

Meanwhile, the amazing mammoth continued to strut its stuff through the Pliocene period for an impressive number of years – surviving from 4.8 million to about 10,000 years ago and ranging from Spain to North America and across to Siberia. All were the proud owners of huge curved tusks. It was the northern species that grew long shaggy hair: these woolly mammoths coped well with the extreme cold of the Ice Age. They had smaller ears than modern elephants and a flap of hairy skin covered the anus, protecting a vital but tender area from the freezing cold. Mammoths had extremely long tusks – up to 16ft (5m)

long. They may well have used these strong, curved ivory tusks as shovels to clear snow from the ground so that they could eat the fresh vegetation buried beneath.

Like many endangered species today, mammoth populations gradually diminished, a situation exacerbated by their numbers being splintered into several small groups thousands of miles apart and therefore more vulnerable to population decline. The last populations teetered on the brink and then finally vanished between 11,000 and 4000 years ago. No-one knows exactly why. They were undoubtedly vulnerable to the early weapons wielded by our own hunting ancestors but they probably also succumbed to the effects of climate change – or fell victim to an infectious disease.

But at least today's elephants are still with us although they are hugely threatened too. However, they continue to serve as a vivid reminder of their ancestors. The *Elephantidae* family is the root from which both mammoth and modern elephants derived and, amazingly, today's Asian elephant is more closely related to the extinct mammoth than it is to its living African counterpart.

Opposite and above: As this representation shows, the prehistoric mammoth of the last Ice Age was unmistakably a relative of the modern elephant – but rather more closely linked to the Asian form, with its small ears and domed head, than to the African elephant.

Physical attributes and how to tell the species apart

While the genetic differences are actually so great that the two species cannot interbreed successfully, the most obvious difference between an African *(Loxodonta africana)* and an Indian elephant *(Elephas maximus)* – and the one most people would quote if pressed for an answer – is that African elephants have enormous ears that extend over the neck and drape over the shoulders measuring 6.6ft (2m) from top to bottom, while Indian elephants have far smaller ears set on dome-shaped heads. But there are many other less-well-known variations that distinguish the African/Asian divide.

The African head flows smoothly without an obvious hump or dent whereas the Asian skull is crumpled from the front to the back, with a domed structure on the top and a dented forehead. Overall, however, the skin of the African elephant is more wrinkled than the Asian's smoother hide. African elephants have proportionally larger eyes and the females, generally, have smoother, flatter heads.

The African elephant is the taller of the two beasts with longer legs and an average height of 9–12ft (3 to 3.65m) with their shoulders marking the highest point. The largest African elephant recorded weighed 27,000lb (12.2 tonnes) and stood 13.8ft (4.2m) high at the shoulder – twice as tall as a human being. The Asian elephant stands a little lower

at 7-11.5ft (2–3.5m) and the top of its head marks the highest point. The weight of an African elephant ranges from 8800–15,500lb (4000 to 7000kg) so they weigh about the same as a single-decker bus. An Asian tips the scales at 6600–11,000lb (3000 to 5000kg).

The African elephant has a straighter or more concave back and has one more vertebra in the lumbar section of its spine than is found in the arched back of its Asian counterpart. An African elephant has up to 21 pairs of ribs while the Asian has up to 20 pairs. Meanwhile, slung underneath this massive body, the belly of the African slopes diagonally downward toward its hind legs; the Asian's stomach is either almost straight or sags in the middle.

Above: The shorter, lighter Asian elephant has small ears, a smoother hide, may have no tusks, longer lower lips and a belly that is straight or sags in the center. Its humped head is its highest point. While African elephants like eating leaves best, their Asian brothers and sisters prefer grass.

Opposite: The taller, heavier African elephant has longer legs, a smoother, flatter head, larger ears and eyes, a straighter or concave back, more ribs and vertebrae, molar teeth with thicker enamel and fewer ridges, more wrinkled skin, differently shaped toes and trunk tips – and a belly that slopes diagonally downward. Its back is its highest point.

Describing elephant feet proves to be surprisingly complicated. Somewhat confusingly, different sources suggest different numbers – both for their toes and for their large, flat nails but this is not as crazy as it at first seems for the toes do, in fact, disappear into the mass of the foot, are mainly internal structures, may be vestigial (now no longer serving their original purpose), and do not all have toenails. The African elephant seems to have four or five 'toes' and nails on its front feet and three on each hind foot. The Asian elephant has five toes and nails on its front feet and three or four on each hind foot. Both have hoof 'slippers' of horny sole.

In outline (as shown distinctly in their footprints) the forefoot is round while the hind foot is oval. When elephants place their weight on their feet, these splay out. When their feet are lifted off the ground, however, their soles bulge outward and downward. This reduction in circumference as the foot is raised makes it far easier for the elephant to pull its foot away from sticky muddy ground.

Elephants do not leave much in the way of tracks because their weight is so well distributed. Their wide, padded feet help elephants to walk quietly but they are also capable of a good turn of speed. When the situation requires them to run, they may reach speeds of 24mph (38kph) over short distances. Their thick soles are cracked and ridged (rather like the sole of a climbing boot) and they provide an excellent grip on steep hills and mountains. When an elephant places a foot on the ground, especially the forefoot, its toes spread and the foot expands to support the weight above. Meanwhile, fatty fibrous tissue acts like a shock absorber as the elephant moves along with its heels raised on this fibrous cushion.

Opposite: Sometimes male Asian elephants lack tusks and certainly it is rare for the females to have them. They are called 'tushes' when they do appear and are visible only if the female opens her mouth. Asian elephants have long been domesticated and have been used for forestry and logging work and as ceremonial animals.

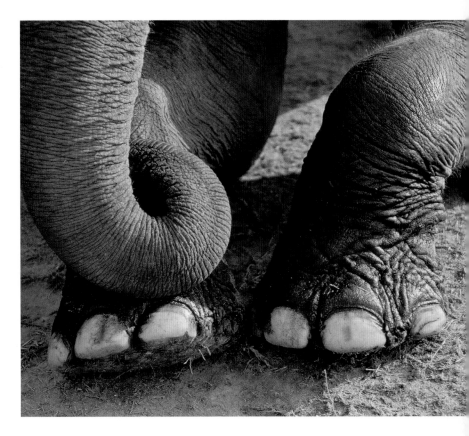

Above and below: The feet of an Asian elephant, above, compared with the foot of an African elephant, below. The only visual evidence of the elephants four or five toes buried within the flesh of the foot are the toe nails, but not all of the toes have nails. The foot is formed in such a way that the elephant is essentially walking on tiptoe.

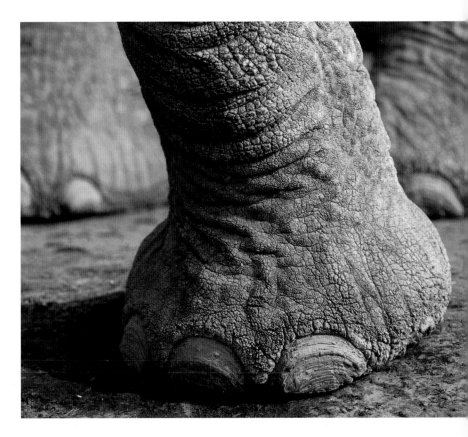

Above: The tusks of African elephants. About one quarter of an elephant's tusk is set within its skull. They grow continuously – about 7in (17cm) each year.

Below: Female Asian elephants grow tushes rather than tusks.

An African elephant's diamond-shaped molar teeth have thicker enamel and fewer, but coarser, ridges than the Asian elephant's strongly compressed molars, which more closely resemble the teeth of the extinct mammoth.

An elephant's tusks are actually elongated upper incisor teeth, which grow continuously throughout its life. The tusks of both male and female African elephants are larger than those of the Asian elephants, whose females may have only rudimentary tusks (called tushes, incisors protruding beyond the upper lip) and sometimes none at all. Only about half the Asian males have proper tusks. Elephants may fight with their tusks but they also use them to scrape bark off trees. Like right- or left-handed humans, elephants are usually right- or left-tusked. The 'master' tusk is subject to greater wear and tear and is generally shorter and more rounded at the tip than the other lesser-used tusk. They use both tusks to dig for water, roots, and minerals, to break branches or maneuver felled tree trunks – and for display and battle.

An African elephant has short, round lower lips; the Asian's lower lips are long and tapering. The African trunk has more rings and is softer and more pliable than the Asian's with two finger-like protuberances at the tip of its trunk that can pick up objects as tiny as a seed or a blade of grass, whereas the Asian elephant has just one projection here. Both use their trunks to drink and to lift food up into their mouths but while African elephants mostly enjoy eating leaves, their Asian counterparts prefer to crop grass.

Opposite and following pages: Most elephants are right- or left-tusked, just as we are right- or left-handed. Tusks wear down with continuous use and sometimes a tusk may be broken during a battle or as a result of an accident, but elephants can survive without them.

Above: *Two Asian elephants with whiskery chins stand trunk to trunk. The elephant order is called Proboscidea – this term deriving from 'proboscis,' which is a word for a long, flexible trunk (or snout). Apart from its immense size, the trunk is probably the feature that most people bring to mind when they think of an elephant.*

Left: *Back in 1975, Pinnawela sanctuary in Sri Lanka was first established as a refuge home for elephants. Here young orphans are cared for and there is now also a breeding program. The large herd that roams here comprises some 60 to 70 animals and includes all age groups from week-old babies to 60-year-olds.*

Right: Close inspection clearly reveals that trunks are not all the same. This one has a pink tinge and is distinctly spotted, as are the tips of the elephant's ears. This is a phenomenon that happens only in Asian elephants. It is thought to be a throwback to the woolly mammoths, and is visible when the skin is free of dust or mud. All elephants use their trunks to rub an itchy eye or scratch an ear, to threaten others and sometimes to throw objects around.

Following pages: This close-up of an African elephant shows the deep cross-hatched pattern of wrinkles on its sandy colored trunk. An elephant drinks by filling its trunk with water and pouring the water down into its mouth.

African forest elephants

These are smaller and stockier than both African savannah and Asian elephants, with darker skin, more rounded ears, hairier trunks, and parallel downward-pointing tusks. They occupy territories measuring about 775sq miles (2000km²) in more deeply forested areas than the savannah elephant would choose to penetrate, and have straighter tusks that are less likely to get snagged in the trees and bushes.

Above: African forest elephants live in dense lowland equatorial forests in west and central Africa where they have created a useful network of trails that benefit other species.

Opposite: When a DNA identification system was set up to trace where poached ivory was coming from, scientists found that the African elephants consisted of two very different species. The forest elephants had found their niche in the equatorial forests where they had lived hidden from view and virtually forgotten.

Above: *An African elephant in confrontational mood is an awesome sight. Generally, elephants are very gentle creatures but a mother will defend her young calf by charging at any intruders and an old male can become very aggressive.*

Keeping their cool

There are differences in temperament too. The Asian elephant is more tractable and more easily tamed to help in forest work, to be ridden and used in ceremonies, and even to perform as a circus animal. The African elephant does not tolerate such interference lightly and has only rarely been used as a working or performing beast, although the Ancient Romans and, famously, the Carthaginians under Hannibal, did train them for use in battle.

For both Asian and African elephants, while dominance, seniority, and rank are directly related to the size and age of

the animals, the temperament of each individual elephant plays its part too and the disciplinary nature of the 'bossier' ones toward others in the herd is a vital element in the establishment of social hierarchy. This begins early with older elephants keeping the younger ones in order.

Keeping cool physically is helped by the elephant's enormous ears. These are covered in veins in unique patterns that can be used to identify individuals rather like our own fingerprints. Because they are packed with blood vessels, when the elephant flaps its ears, they help to lower the body temperature as the rapidly circulating blood passing near the surface of the ears cools down in the breeze.

Above: Asian elephants live in tropical forests, staying deep within the safety of the trees by day and emerging into clearings by night. They are generally placid – timid even – but males become unpredictable and bad-tempered during a period called the musth when their testosterone level is high.

Left: This close-up shows the small ears and wrinkled hide of an Asian elephant: the hotter the climate in which the elephant lives, the less hair it will have. The extinct mammoth had to survive in the freezing conditions of the Ice Age, and so had small hairy ears as well as a shaggy coat.

Following pages: The larger ears of the African elephant make very useful 'air conditioners.' Not only can they be flapped to create a breeze, but they also serve as a natural cooling device through which the blood circulates close to the surface of the skin and is cooled. Elephants do not sweat (except through their toenails) so their ears play a very important role in temperature regulation.

Trunks as tools

The elephant's trunk is a complex structure with radiating muscles arranged like bicycle spokes around each nostril – it comprises about 40,000 muscles with 150,000 associated 'muscle units.' There are no bones to restrict the fluid movement of this veritable 'fifth limb.' It is a versatile tool that serves as nose, arm, hand – and handkerchief. It is powerful enough to kill a lion with a single swipe or lift a 600lb (275kg) weight and yet agile enough to pluck a feather from the ground.

An elephant uses its trunk to pick up plants, graze grass, pick fruit, leaves, or entire branches from trees – and then place these in the mouth. Sometimes they will seize a tree or branch and shake the food down – or simply knock the entire tree over.

An elephant can suck 15 quarts (14 liters) of water into its trunk at a time and then blow the liquid into its mouth. The trunk often serves as a useful snorkel when the elephant is swimming and is a highly developed scent receptor – raised high and swiveled from side to side, it will discover the location of friends, enemies, and food sources. The trunk is used to signal, to greet others, to vocalize, to wipe the eyes (or rub them, or ears, if they itch) and to wrestle. An elephant will attack or defend itself by flailing the trunk at unwanted intruders or even by grasping or throwing them to the ground. The trunk may be used tenderly to comfort and reassure others in the group, and to lift, push, and carry things. When all this becomes too much after a long day, the elephant will rest the weary trunk over its tusk until this vital part of its anatomy has had a chance to recover! If a serious trunk injury should occur, the affected elephant is unlikely to survive.

Right: Two female African elephants stand at the edge of a waterhole with their calves. The youngest baby is suckling. Infants are not fully weaned for several years. As an expression of affection, a mother often pets her baby with her trunk while it nurses.

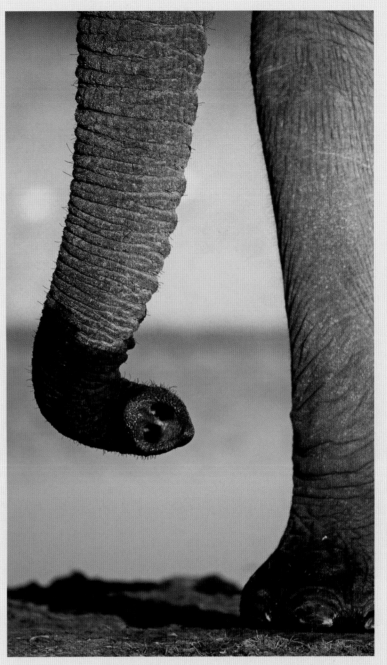

Above: The African elephant's trunk has more rings and is softer and more pliable than the Asian's. With two finger-like protuberances at the tip, it is a remarkably deft limb and can pick up objects as tiny as a seed or feather. It is a complex structure with muscles arranged like bicycle spokes around each nostril.

Left: The trunk can pluck plants, fruit, leaves, or branches from trees and then place them in the mouth. This amazingly versatile tool serves as nose, hand, weapon, and signal apparatus. The trunk is strong enough to kill a lion in one powerful swipe but gentle enough to perform the most delicate movements. Elephants sometimes use their trunks like a handkerchief to wipe their eyes.

Above: *Elephants often greet each other gently, touching and entwining their trunks in their equivalent of a handshake or hug. They may also use their trunks to wrestle and caress. They raise them as a threat signal or lower them to show submission. Trunks can scent the location of food or friends too.*

Opposite: *Elephants can suck up vast volumes of water into their trunks and then blow the liquid back into their mouths to drink, or spray it over their bodies (or each other) if bathing or playing. When swimming, the trunk acts as a breathing tube while its body is submerged underwater.*

Above: *After sucking up many gallons of water this elephant enjoys a welcome cooling shower. It may also spray dust and mud over itself to give its skin a vital protective sunscreen and to reduce the annoyance of biting insects.*

Right: *At the end of the day, a tired elephant often drapes its busy and very heavy 'fifth limb' over one tusk to give this hard-working piece of its anatomy a well-deserved rest!*

Water creatures

Elephants do not jump but they *can* climb and they are amazingly good swimmers. Elephants love water and seek sanctuary from the heat in lakes or rivers, filling their trunks with water and showering themselves to wash off the dust. They are very relaxed in this element – indeed recent research suggests that their trunks may have developed first as underwater breathing tubes before the 'elephant proper' evolved from sea mammals.

Elephant embryos have internal testicles, just like seals and whales, which indicates that they originally inhabited an aquatic environment. Fossil evidence suggests that elephants moved away from aquatic life onto land about 30 million years ago so it is quite possible that when their ancestors lived in water, their trunks may have served as snorkels. Elephants today still use their trunks in this way; their necks are too short to allow them to keep their mouths comfortably above water to breathe when crossing a deep river or lake so they breathe through their raised trunks.

Above and left: Baby elephants learn to swim almost immediately they are born and can even suckle underwater. The youngsters are soon able to enjoy a good splash and a lake or pool makes a cool, inviting playground so long as their mothers keep a watchful look-out for hungry crocodiles.

Above: *Up periscope! Elephants can cross quite deep rushing water by using their trunks as snorkels. Even babies can swim quite strongly and use their trunks to breathe freely when they follow their mothers into deep water.*

When working, Asian elephants often have to travel from one island to another during logging operations. They frequently swim with the trunk up out of the water to breathe – looking rather like a submarine's periscope – and they are able to cope with fast-flowing water in this way. Thailand loggers, for example, take their elephants through quite deep water between the various islands in the Andaman archipelago. Young elephants learn to swim almost immediately and are even able to suckle underwater. The babies use the snorkel technique when they follow their mothers into deep water and find themselves out of their depth. They soon relish the water environment as a cool playground.

Elephants paddle with all four legs to swim and are able to move quite fast, their large bodies providing buoyancy. Among the most able land-dwelling mammal swimmers, they can swim happily for several miles; those near the coast often play in the sea while whole groups will gather in lakes or pools to cavort, splash, flop onto their sides and even roll completely upside down so that only the soles of their feet poke out of the water. Untiring swimmers, they have been known to swim to islands off the coast of India. It could well be that, long ago, elephant ancestors swam to Sri Lanka from India. Adults swim amazing distances almost effortlessly but mothers always keep offspring on the upstream side, shielded from dangerous currents.

Above: Asian working elephants cross from one island to another: elephants can wade through swirling waters or swim swiftly, their large bodies providing buoyancy. In 1989 logging was banned in Thailand – thousands of elephants were suddenly unemployed. Some mahouts moved with their charges into Myanmar (Burma) and other places where elephants continue to work in the industry.

Following pages: An African elephant cools off. Groups often gather at waterholes to quench their thirst and refresh hot bodies.

Staying in contact by trunk and trumpet

The trunk plays a key role in the elephant's social interactions. Those animals who know one another will greet companions by entwining trunks, like a friendly handshake. They also use their trunks to play-wrestle and to caress during courtship. The trunk is a vital element in dominance displays too, being raised as a warning or threat or lowered to signal submission.

Elephant eyes are very small in proportion to their vast heads and contain very few photoreceptors: this means that they cannot see very well beyond a few hundred feet, so an excellent sense of hearing is vital. Elephants make rumbles, growls, bellows, moans, and loud trumpeting noises. They also make sounds that are too low for humans to hear, which can help them to stay in contact over distances of up to a mile or so. Low frequency sounds travel through the ground, like the seismic waves of earthquakes, and they allow the elephants to establish their positions in relation to one another, to co-ordinate group movement, and alert others to their sexual and emotional state.

Above and right: This entangled knot of trunks with many thousands of muscles coming into close contact is the way elephants meet and greet one another, re-establishing contact and friendship.

In fact, the majority of the communication between elephants takes place at the infrasound level (sound with a frequency too low to be detected by humans). An area of up to 20sq miles (50km²) may be covered by these infrasound calls – or up to 39sq miles (100km²) at dusk when the temperatures drop and the sound waves reflect back toward the ground rather than being dissipated into the sky.

Elephants' trunks are packed with vibration sensors and their brains seem to be able to process even very weak signals. Their feet too (and possibly their toenails) are filled with sensors that react to vibrations that ripple through the ground layers and transmit nerve signals to the brain. So, along with chemical signals and all those trumpetings and shrill shrieks, elephants possess an extensive range of communication methods and may be closer to having a true 'language' than we yet understand.

Above and left: *Raising the trunk high up in the air and swiveling it from side to side helps the elephant to interpret vital smells. It also uses its trunk to trumpet loudly when angry, excited, startled – or lost and trying to locate companions. Elephants may scream, cry, bellow, rumble, or snort.*

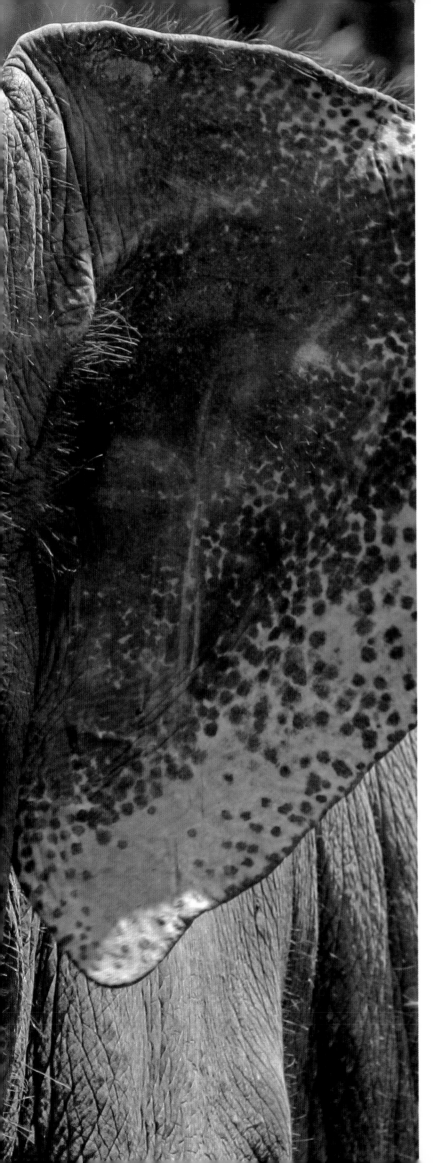

The intelligent elephant

If communication is a measure of intelligence, then elephants certainly qualify as intelligent. Moreover, apart from humans, very few species respond to birth and death so powerfully. Elephants will gather to greet a newborn calf and also mourn lost relatives. Facial, eye and mouth expressions, plus the way they present their ears, heads and bodies, all express emotion. They will tenderly touch the body or handle the bones of a dead elephant. Moreover, when they reach the place where a companion died, they will stop and may maintain a silent vigil for several minutes. They clearly grieve – and understand the concepts of life and loss.

As elephant expert Joyce Poole has observed, elephants are 'self-aware' and can recognize their own reflections in a pool of water – perhaps trying to rub a perceived smudge off the forehead with the trunk. Like apes, they use tools; older matriarchs teach young elephants how to use vegetation to scratch themselves or to remove flies from their bodies. Sometimes they will employ stripped branches as fly swats. They pick up sticks, bones, rocks, or logs to examine – or play with and throw around. Their social intercourse, family bonds, emotion, and intelligence are evident to anyone who is lucky enough to study them closely. These are truly magnificent, highly intelligent creatures.

Left: Now that we know more about elephant communication, we can better appreciate their intelligence. They use many sounds that lie below the range of human hearing but which carry for miles. They stomp their feet and make low rumblings, generating seismic waves that travel through the earth. Such vibrations are thought to be 'received' through their feet. Elephants are also renowned for their remarkable memories.

At Home with the Elephants

Whether an elephant lives among or close to forest trees, on the open savannah, near mountains, or in transit across the desert sands, its home is a precious and fast diminishing habitat. Where once this gentle giant ranged wide, it now survives in scattered pockets of territory. Sadly, despite its great stature – both in terms of scale and in our affections – this amazing animal has become increasingly vulnerable.

An Endangered Giant

Not so long ago – in ecological terms, that is – just a few centuries in the past, African elephants roamed all the savannahs and forests south of the Sahara Desert. But since the explosion in human populations and their dramatic spread into former elephant territory, both savannah and forest have been extensively taken over for agriculture. Elephant habitats shrink daily, and those that remain are scattered – fragmented by human penetration, the work of farmers, and their dwellings.

Meanwhile, Asian elephants, that once ranged from Syria and modern Iraq to the Yellow River in northern China and the islands of Indonesia, are now found only from India to Vietnam with a small population living in captivity in south-west China. The once abundant populations have been reduced to small groups in isolated patches, in tropical savannah, rainforest, tropical deciduous forest, and the Himalayan mountain range.

It is inevitable that those elephants that do survive this devastation of their habitat will wander outside protected areas. Elephants travel great distances in their search for food and also make seasonal migrations. This leads to conflicts between the disparate needs of the farmer and the elephant, especially in places where elephants trample crops in their endless quest for food. Poaching for ivory and hunting for elephant bushmeat, especially in war-torn Central Africa, has taken a heavy toll too – but it is the habitat loss that is increasingly having the greatest impact.

Right: Many factors combine to threaten the elephant's way of life and natural habitat – from forestry to the encroachment of cultivation, irrigation canals and dams, and the scattering of habitat pockets that render traditional migratory routes unviable.

Some scientists now regard the elephant as a 'flagship' species for wider issues on how to manage conservation effectively and recognize the need to create corridors for the free passage of such large mammals as these. In an effort to understand the overall picture, they have begun putting tracking collars on some elephants so that their migrations can be followed by satellite.

In 1930, there were between five and ten million African elephants. By 1979, the number had dropped to 1.3 million. They were added to the international list of the most endangered species by 1989, when only about 600,000 remained, less than one percent of that original number.

Only 30,000 to 40,000 wild Asian elephants survive today, mostly in India (plus some 16,000 domesticated elephants, mainly serving the logging industry). Asian elephants were never as abundant as their African cousins, and now they are even more endangered.

Above: *Elephants browse at the edge of a forest.*

Left: *Amboseli National Park was Kenya's first established game reserve and it boasts the snowcapped peak of Mount Kilimanjaro as one of its major attractions, as well as the variety of wildlife grazing below. In the absence of poaching and culling, the Amboseli elephants have slowly increased in numbers since the late 1970s.*

Following pages: *Elephants enjoy a paddle at the edge of a pool as they drink and top up their hydration levels. Amazingly, an elephant's body is actually 70 percent water!*

Habitats

While most Asian elephants live in forests, staying in the shade among the dense trees and carving out paths between these, some do roam over the open grasslands, marshes, and savannahs in Asia. Others are captive animals, and the pattern of their daily lives has to conform to the dictates of their human owners. Like all elephants, they need regular access to water.

African elephants live mainly on the plains of East Africa but some groups have spread westward into the forests of Central Africa and others have made their homes in small scattered pockets to the west. This type of elephant ranges through the fringes of forest, swamp, and river but by far the greatest numbers inhabit the open savannah – grassland scattered with shrubs and isolated trees, and set between tropical rainforest and a desert environment in a wide band on both sides of the equator. Here their routines adapt to the wet and dry seasons, to days of plentiful water and vegetation, and to those times when vital sustenance becomes a scarce commodity. Too little rain falls here in the dry season to support forests. It is warm all year round, with a very long dry season (when it is actually a little cooler) and a very wet summer season when the stiflingly hot humid air rises to meet the cooler air above and turns into scudding clouds and rain. East African grasslands, such as those in Kenya and the Serengeti region, are sprinkled with acacia trees that provide vital shade for the elephants.

African forest elephants (*Loxodonta cyclotis*) live in small numbers in the dense rainforests of the Congo Basin, close to the equator where it is very warm and wet, while Asian elephants are mainly forest animals, and prefer to stay in the shade in the different types of wooded environment in South-East Asia, which include dry thorn forests, floodplains, and tropical forests.

Elephants are also seen on mountain slopes, albeit below the snowline, in regions such as the Himalayas and around Mount Kilimanjaro in Africa.

Right: Here we see a trio of elephants in a grassland and scrub environment. These herbivores consume between 100 and 500 species of plants, including grasses, trees, vines, and shrubs.

Life in the desert

By contrast, other African elephants make their home in the parched deserts of western Niger and the Etosha Pans of Namibia, seeking some shade in the dense thickets of tamarisk and acacias that line the river beds. They have adapted to this harsh environment by conserving energy and drinking frugally from ephemeral rivers (which become damp river beds when the water evaporates) and scattered waterholes – sometimes slaking their thirst only every third or fourth day. During the rains they enjoy grazing on abundant grass so the woody plants have a chance to recover and then, once the dry season arrives, they browse on different woody species.

Although these elephants do break branches like other elephants, they are not nearly so destructive as forest or savannah elephants and seldom fell trees or strip them of bark so devastatingly. Furthermore, the broken debris of branches or felled trees left in their wake often creates a sheltered place on the ground where grass plants are protected from the harsh sun and from other animals that might graze here or trample them underfoot. Meanwhile, the successfulness of the germination of some tree seeds, such as acacias, is actually enhanced by them passing through the elephants' digestive system as the enzymes in the digestive juices break down the hard outer seed coat, allowing moisture to penetrate once they are excreted in the animal's dung.

Left: Considering the vast expanse of the Namibia desert stretching all around, this herd is passing incredibly close to the scattered dwellings of a Himba village in Kaokoland.

Opposite: Elephants on the march across a terrain of dry bleached grass, with the young ones closely protected every step of the way.

Following pages: Here zebras watch as the herd passes through African grassland. During the rainy season, over half of the elephants' food will consist of new grasses but as these dry out in the hot sun, they will look for fruit to eat and also browse on shrubs.

Altering the habitat

Elephants make a phenomenal impact on whatever landscape they inhabit as they forge trails, debranch or demolish trees, break up dense bushes, create salt licks and gouge out waterholes. This process is not entirely destructive – they change their surroundings undoubtedly, but can also lay the foundation for grasslands to develop. Meanwhile, other smaller animals depend upon the openings that elephants create in the forest and brush – and even humans have used these tracks as the foundation for roads. Other animals are also only too happy to quench their thirst at any vital waterholes the elephants have dug.

Because of this, and their destruction of trees, elephants are called a keystone species – a term which means that they have a disproportionately large effect on their environment relative to their actual abundance. They are able to radically alter the habitat in which they, and many other species, spend their lives.

Above: Elephants really enjoy eating many parts of a tree – twigs, bark, blossom, fruit, and leaves. The elephant tears branches off the tree by putting its trunk around them and twisting hard.

Opposite: Elephants have a huge impact on the environment. Some people regard their destruction of trees as a negative influence, but in fact it provides young grass, plants, and saplings with a chance to develop – their growth is enhanced by the new thrust of sunlight. Grasslands depend upon the elephant for their survival.

Below: The silhouette of tree with a large bird perched atop its thorny foliage. Elephants often seek shelter from the sun under the shadow cast by the umbrella of an acacia tree. Moreover, when the trees bear fruit, elephants help to spread the seeds far and wide by eating the pods. The seeds pass through their digestive system and the warm dung provides a rich environment in which they can germinate.

Finding food

Such a massive animal has a huge appetite and requires an immense habitat to satisfy this. Elephants spend up to 18 hours of each day eating. They use up enormous amounts of energy and need a constant intake of food to fuel their daily needs, especially as they digest only about 40 percent of what they consume. They often have to travel many miles to find sufficient supplies for the herd to survive. Each day, as they make their hungry way through vast areas of grasses, trees, and shrubs, about three-quarters of their waking time is spent munching away at the juiciest leaves they can find on trees and shrubs, as well as cropping grass, shoots, small branches and twigs, thorns, bark, fruits and pods, buds and flowers, seeds, roots, bulbs and tubers – and drinking tree sap.

These vigorous – and occasionally overenthusiastic – diners will often uproot and scatter as much as they consume, sometimes even smashing down trees entirely. However, while elephants may pull down trees to obtain tasty treats from the top, they are also quite capable of delicately plucking a single berry from a high branch.

Above and right: An elephant spends much of its day eating a rich variety of foods including grass, flowers, roots, bulbs and shoots, as well as various parts of trees including the vital bark that provides it with essential minerals and nutrients.

Sometimes they bend down the trees with their large heads and bodies so that they can reach the leaves from the topmost branches as these are the sweetest ones that they enjoy most of all. Even when they do break off branches, other smaller mammals can benefit from this scattering of juicy treetops at a level they can now reach.

Grass is the easiest of the items on the menu for the elephant to digest but eating a wider range of vegetation ensures more balanced nutrition. There can be dangers in an overzealous attempt to grub up bulbs from hard ground or smash trees, however, as elephant tusks do sometimes break. Generally, it is the sweetest-tempered male elephants

that retain the largest and, paradoxically, most fierce-looking tusks – because these more gentle beasts are less likely to indulge in combat and tree ramming.

Elephants usually eat about 180kg (400lb) of vegetation each day (sometimes much more). This seems a lot but in proportion to their body weight elephants actually eat less than mice. They also need large quantities of water – both to quench their thirst and for bathing. To meet the demands of living in a hot climate, they must drink around 135–225 litres (30 to 50 gallons) of water every day – and often more. Their trunks act as large hoses, with a capacity of between 4–10 litres (7 to 18 pints).

The elephant keeps constantly on the move, looking for the necessary supply of food and sources of water. Not so long ago, they could follow age-old seasonal migration routes from one habitat to another but now they often find that these ancient routes lead them into unprotected areas where danger threatens. Unfortunately, moreover, some resourceful elephants in patches of forest that have become isolated and, where the supplies have started to dwindle, have resorted to raiding local villages for food and water, relishing juicy farm crops of fruits and vegetables. These thefts can ultimately lead to the elephants' demise as they are hunted by the aggrieved villagers.

Above: Elephants strip trees of bark as well as pushing them over – and they often pull up plants, rather than simply grazing. After laying waste to an area they move on. Sadly, in today's restricted elephant zones, the landscape has less time for the cycle of regeneration to catch up and repopulate it with plants in their wake.

Opposite: Elephants often stand on their hind legs to crop the treetops, and will also sometimes uproot and push trees over. Here a herd has completely destroyed an acacia tree.

Above: *An elephant's trunk can pluck tender leaves and fruit very gently from a tree. In forest areas, elephants travel relatively slowly, eating the available plants and foliage as they move across some 3 miles (5km) each day. This individual has lost a tusk – perhaps while forcefully uprooting a tree.*

Left: *Because their territories are now so much more restricted, the elephants are capable of destroying trees and vegetation at a faster rate than the plants are able to recover.*

Following pages: *Trunks are highly flexible cropping and dining tools. Those elephants that live in areas of mixed woodland and grasslands spend the hottest part of the day in the shade of the trees and then graze in the grassland once the temperature drops.*

The dung heap

Of the 330 to 440lb (150–200kg) of green food that an elephant crops each day, 80 percent is converted into fertile manure. They can pass droppings about 18 times a day, at least once an hour. Over 50 percent of what they eat comes straight out the other end and many animals (including birds, mammals, insects, baboons, and monkeys) find useful food in this dung. They follow the elephant trail for such pickings, searching through the droppings to find undigested seeds and nuts.

Flies, beetles, and worms also seek nourishment in elephant dung. Dung beetles especially revel in these fresh droppings. Scientists have counted more than 7000 in a single bolus and up to 16,000 dung beetles (*Scarabaeidae*) have been estimated to be busy in a 3.30lb (1.5kg) heap of elephant dung. The beetles shovel the dung into their mouths, squeeze it, and swallow the juices before squeezing again and swallowing the solid parts. Some dung beetles also find the material they need for their nests in these deposits and even meet their mates in a delicious dung pat. The male offers the female a giant-sized brood ball; if she accepts this, they then roll it away together – or the female may hitch a ride on top. Other beetles often attempt to steal

the spherical prize. Once the elephant dung ball is securely buried, the female of the pair lays an egg there. The protective female dung beetle stays with the dung ball and her grub for about two months.

While cattle dung may be the first choice for some scarab beetles, about 100 dung beetle species use elephant dung either primarily or exclusively to stock their nests and thus help to clean up the ground – and to keep it fertilized. Termites also carry elephant fecal matter below ground and so they too help to keep the soil aerated and distribute the valuable nutrients. This splendid and plentiful manure is full of nutrient-rich material that improves poorer soils.

Above left: In some countries a number of paper products are now made from elephant dung, which is full of fiber.

Above right: Some dung beetles make their nests from elephant dung. The male offers his mate a giant-sized brood ball and they may then roll this away together.

Opposite: The research of some scientists suggests that the amount of dung an elephant deposits is related to the rainfall levels in the preceding two months and the subsequent availability of food.

Keeping comfortable

Africa and Asia can be very hot and so elephants really enjoy cooling off in lakes or rivers whenever the opportunity arises. Elephants can smell water over 5.5 miles (9km) away and will travel great distances in search of this vital resource. When the dry season takes its toll and bakes the ground, they can live without water for nearly two weeks. Elephants suck up water with their trunks and then, after drinking their fill, they will splash themselves with water and mud and wash their babies. Sometimes they appear to be simply enjoying themselves, seeming playful and obviously revitalized once they have cooled off. Water serves an important role in helping the elephants to avoid heat exhaustion because they have no major sweat glands to help regulate their body temperature through the cooling effect of sweating.

They splash and squirt water and roll about in it: both adults and youngsters play and frolic, wallowing in the shallows or sometimes submerging completely in deep water. If they have cooled off by rolling in soft mud, once they emerge the mud will dry on their skins – and it thus creates a barrier against the scorching sun. Even in arid desert areas, elephants will seek out precious reservoirs, using their tusks and trunks to dig down into dry river beds to find the precious liquid. They hand down the knowledge of such important places from one generation to another.

Above and below: A young African elephant will cool off by playing and splashing in muddy water. The mud will then dry on its skin and protect it from the sun and irritating insects. The encrusted mud cakes bone dry and then falls off, taking away with it a good crop of ticks at the same time.

Opposite: Elephants can scent the presence of water from many miles away. They need to bathe frequently, not only to cool down but also to help wash away disease-carrying parasites.

At other times they will take dust baths to reduce the irritation of insect bites, throwing dust over their itchy backs. Their skin is surprisingly sensitive to sunburn and insect attack, and both mud and dust serve to protect their hides from the hot sun and from biting insects. The color of the mud in which they wallow can turn them different hues – black or even yellow or rust red, as in Tsavo National Park in Kenya.

Meanwhile, they regularly flap their ears to help blood circulation, which keeps them even cooler. The Asian elephant probably evolved with smaller ears because it stays in the shade for most of the time and does not need the

large areas of radiating skin that the African elephant does.

An elephant's skin has many wrinkles that increase the surface area that soaks up water when they bathe and also traps precious moisture for when they emerge. During the hottest part of the day, they may take a short snooze – sometimes standing up and sometimes lying down.

Above: A pair of well-submerged elephants revel in the cooling deep water, washing away dust and becoming shiny and clean again.

Following pages: Here an Asian working elephant wades through deep water. Washing, bathing, and having a good splash is part of the daily routine of the working elephant.

Above: *This elephant has blown a veritable cloud of dust over its back. Just like mud, a coating of dust protects against sunburn and repels insects. Often the waterhole routine is first a drink, then a mud bath, and finally a dust bath.*

Right: *An elephant stirs up the dust with a sweeping movement of its trunk, then sucks it up, flips its trunk up over its head and blows great clouds that cascade down over its back. This extra protective layer is especially important in the open savannah where there is less shade and the sun can really scorch exposed skin.*

Following pages: *Tsavo National Park, where these elephants are found, is well known for the myth of its 'red elephants,' for herds here do appear to be a wonderful rust red color after taking dust baths in a land where the soil is a glorious orange.*

Above: *Elephants will dig to find water during dry seasons, discovering water sources that still flow under dry river beds and sand. Thus they create vital new waterholes and develop a crucial resource for the whole ecosystem – not just for the elephants themselves.*

Opposite: *Elephants need to find water in order to avoid heat exhaustion. They enjoy wallowing in the shallows and are quite clearly revitalized and playful once they have cooled off. Here they are paddling in a Sri Lankan river.*

Following pages: *A family group slakes its thirst. The herd is nervous when moving into open areas and must ensure the young ones are safe from attack by crocodiles, lions, or spotted hyenas.*

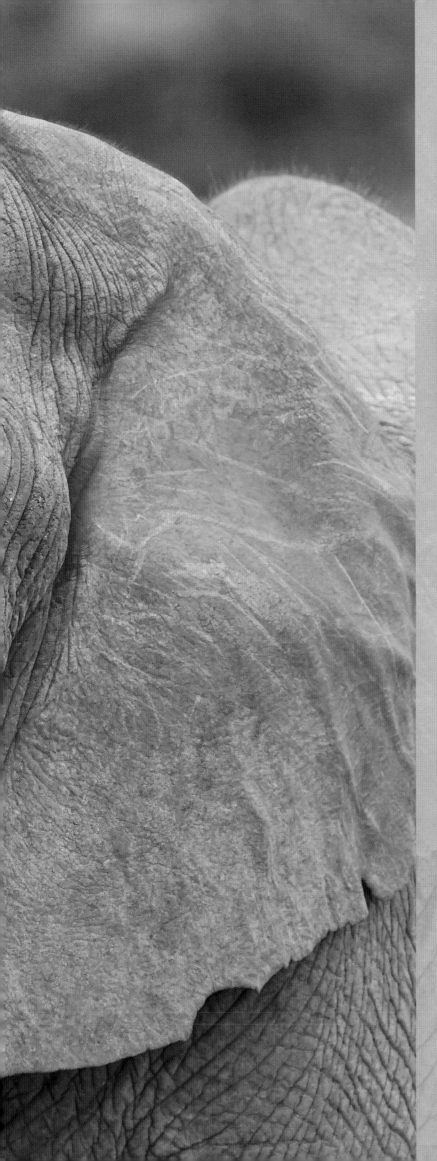

Above: *An elephant squirts water into its mouth with a trunk that can suck up 8 to 10 pints (4 to 5 liters) at a time. It pours this copious draft of water down its throat, tilting its head slightly to make this operation easier. The trunk is very flexible, containing more than 40,000 muscles.*

Left: *The trunk is as supple as a garden hose because it is made of muscle and tendon, not bone. An elephant changes the sound of its call by altering the shape of its nostrils.*

Finding salt and other minerals

The plants that elephants consume do not contain all the minerals they need in sufficient quantities to maintain optimum health. In some places, at 'salt licks' where the soil contains the necessary salts to make up for these deficiencies, elephants will dig deep into the ground – as do deer and other herbivores. They all visit these special places to procure vital supplements to their diets. However, the term 'salt lick' is a misnomer as they cannot actually *lick* up the salt – elephants' tongues are not long enough to reach around their trunk and tusks – so they gouge out the salt with their tusks (which can eventually be worn down to stumps), and then scoop it up with their trunks. Finally, they grind up the lumps with their great molar teeth, before swallowing them.

Above: Elephants are social beings who gather together – to eat, drink, wash, and swim. Sometimes they also congregate at salt licks where they top up their mineral intake.

Right: Forest elephants dig with their tusks and trunks for mineral-rich mud in a waterhole at Dzanga Bai clearing, Dzanga-Ndoki National Park, Central African Republic. It is believed the mud not only supplements their diet but also neutralizes toxins.

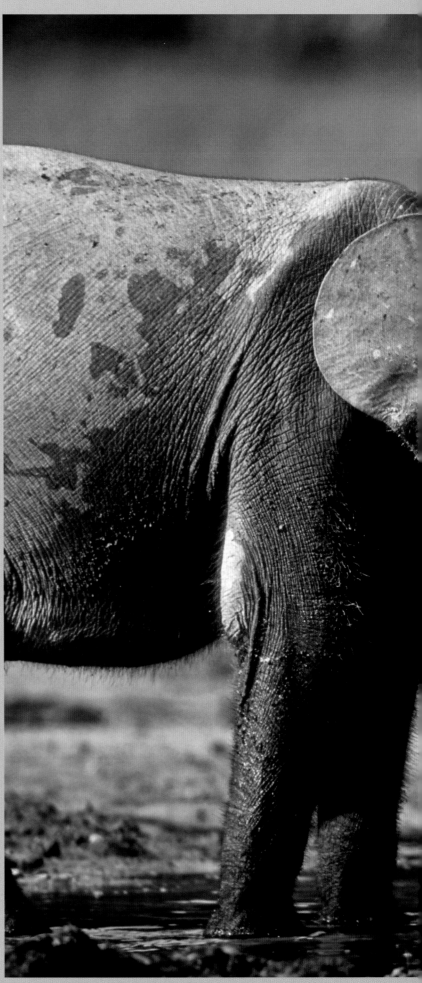

Elephants also dig for minerals in cave walls. For example, at Mount Elgon in Kenya, elephants have been observed finding their way through the pitch-black darkness, negotiating deep crevasses and rockfalls. Ever at risk of being preyed upon by opportunist hyenas or leopards, they seek a passage to where the volcanic agglomerate in the cave walls is rich in minerals. These include the sodium ions elephants need – and they are present here at over a hundred times the level found in the plants they eat. Moreover, it seems that the mineral harvest is even richer the farther inside the cave they penetrate. Recent research suggests that the droppings of the tongue-clicking fruit bats, which live in the depths of the cave, react with the rocks of the floor to form an especially mineral-rich crust.

Above: *A trio of African elephants drink side by side: during the dry season. When water is low, an elephant will dig holes to find hidden sources of water in underground springs.*

Left: *African elephants take a refreshing break in a shallow pool. As the dry season advances, water levels dwindle and natural friends and foes are forced to gather together to drink and bathe. Some waterholes will eventually vanish altogether.*

Above: African and Asian elephants seek natural sources of vital minerals, such as sodium. This elephant is covered in a dusting of white salt.

Right: Elephants need minerals as well as water and may visit salt licks to supplement the intake they obtain from their natural diet. Although scientists have yet to prove this, it seems that sometimes females do so more enthusiastically, spending more time at salt licks perhaps to satisfy increased nutritional needs during pregnancy or when feeding an infant.

Following pages: Elephants reflected in a pool. We now know that elephants do recognize themselves in a mirror — this is a very rare instance of self-awareness in the animal world.

A future home

The more we learn about elephants, the more important it seems that we should care enough to save these intelligent creatures from extinction and make strenuous efforts to ensure their survival. If we wish to continue to delight in elephants' many amazing characteristics and to share this globe meaningfully with them, we must secure both the animals' own future and that of the places where these great creatures live and breed. We must maintain the ecological integrity of their environment. We must make sure that the elephant continues to have, not just sanctuary, but a real viable home in our world.

Above and right: Elephants are such very special creatures. Of course, every species is unique and has individual qualities, but the elephant really is one of a kind like no other, both in terms of its sensitivity and intelligence, as well as its amazing size and appearance.

The Herd

The **herd** usually comprises some eight to 15 **female** elephants and their **calves** led by the **oldest**, largest, most **dominant** one – a stern but kind **matriarch** who watches out for all **members** of the group in her charge. Apart from the **young** male calves that will **leave** as they **mature**, the herd will stay **together** for life and forms an intimate close-knit **society**.

Learning and Experience

With the exception of humans, elephants have the largest brain size – in proportion to their body weight – of any mammal. An elephant's brain weighs just over 11lb (5kg). Whales are known to be highly intelligent but while their bodies are many times larger than that of an elephant (an adult African elephant weighs about the same as a blue whale's tongue), the elephant brain is proportionally much greater at 0.08 percent of the total body weight, whereas the blue whale's brain is just 0.00017 percent of its body weight.

The largest portions of an elephant's brain are responsible for hearing, smell and coordination of movement and another sizeable segment is involved with the interpretation of messages picked up by their highly sensitive trunks. The temporal lobe (responsible for hearing and language) is, relatively, far greater in size than that of dolphins or humans – in the herd, of course, good communication is vital.

Moreover, the growth of an elephant's brain, as it learns and develops, allows for expansion. Except for primates, most mammals are born with a brain weighing already 90 percent of its adult weight. A human brain at birth, however, is a mere 26 percent of its ultimate adult weight and it will grow to be a far greater proportion – and will develop as new behaviors are learned.

Right: *The security of the herd is essential to offer protection and the opportunity for a long learning period while the vulnerable youngsters discover what being an elephant means.*

A baby elephant's brain is only 35 percent of the weight of an adult brain, so while there is not quite so much proportional growth as with the human brain, there is a far greater percentage of development than with most other mammals. These statistics suggest that the elephant will attain a high level of intelligence and that a great deal of learning will take place as the elephant develops from birth to maturity.

This large brain certainly allows the elephant to exhibit the wide range of skills and understanding necessary to be 'part of the team' – playful behavior, sympathetic responses such as grief, artistic skills, self-awareness, a phenomenal memory, and the use of tools. The intelligent elephant communicates with others through scent, a broad range of sounds, and touch.

Left and above: These much-loved youngsters encapsulate the future of the herd. They will reach puberty at 10 to 15 years of age, and will be fully mature at about 20. They achieve their full mental capacity when 30 to 45 years old.

A matriarchal society

Elephants live in a complex matriarchal society where the herd size ranges from five to 30 individuals but usually comprises some eight to 15 family members – of various sizes and ages – led by a dominant female, generally the oldest, largest one. With the exception of the immature male calves, this is a female society, a well-bonded unit that will stay together for life under the control of a stern but kind matriarch who watches out for all the herd. If a member has strayed and makes distress noises to say it is lost, it will be the matriarch who answers. She is the dominant grandmother, who makes all the decisions for the family and is unlikely to be challenged. In sharp contrast to some of the male-dominated societies in the animal world, elephant cow leaders rarely spar with other elephants.

Three or four generations of cows (plus calves) will spend their entire lives together in this intimate family group that, in turn, can be subdivided into two types of family unit – one comprises cows who are nursing calves, and the other includes the non-lactating cows and weaned youngsters.

Troops that are related ('kin' or 'bond' groups) will stay in relatively close range of each other and come together regularly as members of an extended family – often gathering to drink at a watering hole. They communicate a good deal and sometimes link up to form larger bond groups. They may even join forces to create clans of over 200 members, especially if threatened in any way. During the wet season, in particular, elephants may gather as a 'superherd' in vast numbers, sometimes communicating through low frequency sounds that they transmit over very long distances.

Right: The matriarch makes all the decisions and will lead the herd until she is 55 to 60 years old. She understands her environment, knows the herd's routes intimately, keeps a wary eye out for danger, and is a great fount of knowledge as well as a strong, wise leader.

Above: *If the herd is threatened, the elephants will group together and surround the calves to protect them from danger. The matriarch may then decide to confront the threat or to lead the closely gathered herd away to safety.*

The stability and identity of these groups mutate according to the environmental conditions and/or any threats that arise. Family groups link consistently with other family units to which they are probably related, and all the young elephants play together and learn as they do so, creating strong bonds with calves of a similar age and, thus, with the other calves' family groups.

The wise matriarchs know their environment better than younger leaders and head up the most successful herds, always keeping a wary eye out for danger. Moreover, they are better at distinguishing the calls of familiar herds, which saves a good deal of time-wasting and potential dispute

when other elephants come to call. So when an older, experienced matriarch is slaughtered by human hunters, who are attracted by her large size, the herd loses a huge store of knowledge and the skills of a vital leader who had determined the group's direction and pace.

Eventually, however, even the wisest matriarch becomes too old to continue leading the herd successfully (usually when aged between 55 to 60 years). She will then be replaced by her next-in-line, the second-oldest female. A matriarch that is ill or injured badly may also be replaced. Whatever the circumstances, once her rule is over, she either leaves the herd or is abandoned.

Above: *Mothers and young calves remain in constant contact. This is a very intimate relationship, backed up by the strength of the herd whose members all share in the joy of a new arrival and combine forces whenever greater protection for the young is needed.*

Above: *Three or four generations of cows from the same family spend their entire lives in a herd that is split into two units: one comprises cows nursing calves and the other the non-lactating cows and weaned youngsters. The close bond between mother and daughter may last for over 50 years.*

Right: *Mother elephants somehow manage not to tread on or trip over their tiny calves as the youngsters gambol between their enormous pillar-like legs. The females touch their youngsters gently with their trunks and legs and will push them underneath their bellies to protect them from predators or the hot sun.*

Meeting and greeting

A young calf often places the tip of its trunk in its mother's mouth, especially when nervous or stressed. As elephants mature, this close contact develops into a greeting activity, with a lower-ranking animal inserting its trunk tip into the mouth of an approaching adult. Other greeting activities include trunk twining, touching, embracing, caressing, and rubbing – all activities first acquired during the period when a calf bonds with its mother and then the herd.

When related elephant groups meet, they clearly recognize each other at a distance. They will exhibit a great excitement as they all gather together again, and individuals greet old friends with obvious and intense pleasure – even after a relatively short absence. They run toward each other, trumpeting, bellowing, and raising their heads in the air, as well as making contact calls with sounds that are inaudible to human ears. Once they meet, they will click tusks, intertwine trunks, and rumble and growl loudly. They will also flap their ears and hold these in the greeting position. Rather less endearingly, they may urinate and defecate for a riotous ten minutes or so.

Left: A calf peeps out from the curve of its mother's protective encircling trunk. If a calf does wander off to play and confronts a threat, it will squeal in fear – at which point its mother and other herd members will instantly rush to help and protect it.

Following pages: The trunk plays an important part in elephant meeting and greeting rituals and an amazing variety of different trunk contacts will be displayed as well as a good deal of trumpeting, rumbling, ear flapping, and tusk clicking.

Raising the offspring

For its first two years, an elephant infant drinks its mother's milk – a rich source of nourishment and vitamins. Then, although still enjoying some milk from its mother for the next three years or more, the young calf begins to supplement its diet with vegetable matter. By the time it is about five years old, the next young sibling will have arrived and the youngster must now become a little more independent.

Few cow elephants with a calf to suckle have sufficient milk to feed two youngsters so if a calf is orphaned before it is two, it is unlikely to survive, however much the herd family tries to love and care for it. No cow will jeopardize the future of her own calf by feeding another and an orphaned infant without milk will soon grow weak. As its strength diminishes, it will be unable to keep up with a herd that marches ever onward. The decision of the matriarch is always final and an orphan must be abandoned if caring for it will place the rest of the troop at risk. However, there may occasionally be a happier outcome when a mother that has lost her baby – or whose youngster is almost independent – will allow an orphaned infant to suckle.

Above: Affectionate 'trunk huging' is a physical form of communication that youngsters learn from other members of the herd.

Right: It takes many weeks of practice before a baby elephant is able to master the complexities of drinking water using its trunk.

The young elephant forms a very strong social bond with its mother, and also with its brothers and sisters, as they all play together and copy and learn from each other. They will walk and rest, feed and drink, and wallow, wash, and swim as a unit – usually keeping very close to one another all day. Young cow elephants soon learn all about elephant-style motherhood 'on the job' as they help to raise the rest of the family. It seems that elephants do need role models and it has been observed that orphaned elephants placed in reserves do not acquire the right elephant skills unless adult elephants are there to instruct them in appropriate herd behavior.

Calves are very playful, especially when there is water around to add to the fun. They play alone or with other youngsters, the males especially enjoying a good deal of trunk wrestling, shoving, and butting, as they learn to assess one another's fighting abilities and strength.

Opposite and above: Mothers help their infants discover the world around them. However, the calves are cared for not only by their mothers but also by aunts, sisters, and cousins who act as nannies or babysitters in this extended family. In the process, young females learn much that will help them in their future role as mothers.

Left: By the time a young elephant is about five years old it will become more independent of its mother and find its appropriate place in the hierarchy of the herd.

Above: Calves are introduced to water at a very early age and, as they imitate their elders, soon discover the joy of swimming.

Above: Not until they are about four months old do calves really begin to experiment with their trunks; it will take a lot of practice before the calf can control all those muscles and master the full repertoire of intricate trunk movements. Meanwhile, there can be many frustrating setbacks. It often trips up when its trunk gets in the way of its feet, particularly while playing in the slippery mud.

Above: *A young elephant soon learns that the trunk plays a key role in communication. A raised trunk can signify a warning or a threat, while a lowered trunk is often a sign of submission.*

Left: *Young elephants learn through play, discovering how to use their limbs and trunks and exploring their physical strength as they wrestle, romp, charge, and scramble on top of one another.*

A male elephant's life

When a young male reaches puberty (at about a dozen years of age) he will gradually leave the security of his birth herd. Initially, he simply spends more time at the edge of the group, gradually roaming farther afield on his own – for hours, and then days, at a time. Understandably some prove a little reluctant to set off out into the big wide world alone and do not 'make a clean break.' Instead, they stay close to their family herd for several years, sometimes being chased away and made to keep their distance. Eventually, days of independence turn into weeks, and at about 14 years of age, the young bull finally leaves for good. He may range as a solitary bull or become one of a pair of young males, or join a small group, or seek full membership of a bachelor gang of roaming males.

Above and right: An African male in his prime. This solitary giant is a daunting sight as he stands some 13ft (4m) high.

Now separated from his family group, it is time for the young elephant to 'apprentice himself' to the high-ranking bulls in order to learn the codes of behavior that govern the lives and social interaction of adult males. Meanwhile, the youngsters associate freely with one another and are not aggressive toward other wandering bulls. Males in bachelor herds may fight for dominance but, when sexually inactive, stay in smaller 'rest zones,' often with a few companions.

An elephant reaches his prime in his thirties and forties when he is still strong and healthy. Ultimately, the fully mature male bull chooses a mainly solitary life and will challenge other bulls over rank – even when drinking water. Bulls wander farther than cows, only occasionally associating with other males, and with females in heat. Only the most dominant males will be permitted to mount the receptive females. Meanwhile, the lower-ranking bulls must wait their turn to mate while the 40–50-year-old bulls dominate both the battle and the breeding scene.

Fights can be very fierce and prolonged; one battle between two elephants was recorded as lasting 10 hours and 56 minutes but a lot of this apparent aggression, posturing, and noise is bluff. Serious injuries are rare. Highly aggressive displays generally persuade the younger, or smaller, or more timid protagonist to retreat before he suffers any real damage.

Sometimes, however, when the breeding season is at its peak at what is called the *musth* (a word derived

from a Persian term for intoxicated), highly aggressive confrontations may lead to injury. The bull, hoping to impress the females, hangs around, ever optimistic that he will find a receptive mate, and is now so 'psyched up' that he will fight almost any other male he meets. Meanwhile, a powerful odor advertises his excited state as he leaves his scent on trees and other landmarks. A thick flow of sticky fluid dribbles downs his cheeks (indicating his state of musth) and his great wrinkled forehead vibrates as low-frequency rumbles, inaudible to humans, advertise his readiness to mate to other elephants far and wide.

An elephant may be considered to be past his absolute prime when he reaches his fifties – and to be old once his sixtieth year is reached. Very old bulls can become lonely, irritable, and unpredictable – vast ponderous hulks with enormous tusks, they often end their days gazing at the world from tired eyes as they graze in swampy areas where they can still consume great quantities of herbage as their last molars are worn away. When the ancient teeth finally prove incapable of chewing even the softest material, death will swiftly quench the old giant's hunger pangs.

Above and opposite: *Sparring males take one another's measure as they grapple, stirring the dust as they test each other's mettle with clashing tusks. However, they rarely inflict serious injuries.*

Above: *A mature male elephant surveys the savannah. Young males leave the herd in their 'teenage' years to live alone or join a bachelor herd until the strongest and most dominant males earn the right to mate.*

Left: *A male elephant reaches his prime in his thirties and forties when he is mature, strong, and healthy. Here, a threatening bull stands with his legs planted firmly apart and his ears spread wide, ready to deal with any challenge.*

Above: *Elephants lock trunks to test each other's strengths and weaknesses. This all looks very fierce but most of the bouts of pushing are for display or to 'sound out' the opposition rather than real determined aggression. There is ample opportunity for a younger, weaker, or less confident elephant to back off safely.*

Right: *When a bull is in full musth (the period in its hormonal cycle when testosterone levels are at their highest), if he is not hovering around the female herds seeking a receptive mate, he will engage in physical combat with almost any other male he meets.*

Following pages: *Male elephants in their prime and in later life can be fierce and unpredictable at times.*

Postures and threats

A confident elephant will stand tall and proud, with head and tail raised, ears spread, and trunk relaxed. However, when it is necessary to show dominance, the head will be raised higher and the trunk will assume a sharper angle.

When a mild threat is required, such as when a female wants to remind others of her rank, she assumes an alert posture and will turn her body or head toward any other elephants that approach and will nod with ears half spread.

A stronger threat merits fully spread ears while head, tail, and trunk are raised or turned to detect any useful scent indicators. There may be some head tossing, with the head first lowered, then raised sharply and lowered again – slowly. Head shaking and twisting is another option as great ears slap against wrinkled faces.

Above: To those who 'know their elephants,' the animal's stance imparts a lot of information. How the bulk of the body is held plus the angle of head, ears, tail, and trunk convey both mood and rank.

Right: The fully spread ears, curling trunk, and confident demeanor of this mother elephant indicate her determination to defend the calf who presses against her side for reassurance.

Above: *Displacement activities to avoid direct confrontation include swaying, swinging a foot, pawing the ground, or throwing dust about. Meanwhile the trunk may be swished from side to side and waved around energetically.*

Opposite: *Elephants of either sex may engage in a game of friendly sparring. An evenly matched pair of males will trunk-wrestle and push one another, while making noisy growls, roars, screams, and trumpetings. This show of strength and aggression may ultimately develop into a ramming fight.*

Left: *An African elephant makes a threat display by lowering its head and flaring out its ears. An angry elephant will trumpet loudly and blow sharp gusts of air down its trunk. Branches, bushes, and grass may be torn up and thrown at an intruder.*

If this fails to deter the interloper, then the trunk may be swished – or furled up and then unrolled like a curly party 'whizzer,' as the elephant trumpets loudly and blows a sharp gust of air down its trunk (human interference sometimes invites this particular display). Meanwhile branches, bushes, and grass may be torn up and hurled at an intruder.

The next stage is to effect a swift mock charge with ears spread wide, head held high, tail out, while blaring out a warning trumpet. This looks very intimidating, although it is usually only for show as the elephant stops short and then moves away at an angle, looking back at the culprit with its head held high, back arched, and tail raised.

However, if the threat is considered serious, the charge will not be merely for show. It will hurtle onward with serious results for the offender. An enraged or vindictive elephant can wreak havoc, especially if it is a rogue elephant – a lone, violently aggressive giant.

When a pair of elephants are about to fight – whether as a matter of ritual, as a game, or to embark on a really serious battle between rival males – the two contenders will first take one another's measure, with their heads held really high, and their tusks or trunk bases linked together. Generally, the taller elephant dominates, especially if its tusks prove larger and more impressive.

If the pair are evenly matched, then they may move onto the pushing and trunk-wrestling stage, accompanied by noisy growls that can rise in a crescendo of battle cries – roars, screams, and trumpeting. If this is a serious battle over a female, a ramming fight may ensue. With discretion often proving the better part of valor, however, submission is an acceptable escape route and can be indicated by flattened ears, while the loser judiciously backs up or turns away from the victor – or simply runs swiftly away.

Displacement activities may also be a way to avoid direct confrontation and can include touching the temporal gland, rubbing an eye, swaying, swinging a foot, pawing the ground, or throwing dust about. An exaggerated form of feeding behavior can also serve to divert attention and may include breaking off branches, or pulling up and slapping grass against the foot.

Dealing with predators

The herd is constantly on the move and often exposed to dangers but the adults will immediately rally round to protect the little ones if a threat is detected, such as a prowling lion or tiger. Other predators include hyenas, leopards, crocodiles, and, sadly, humans who have long hunted elephants, often seeking their fine ivory tusks as trophies or for commercial gain.

An adult elephant's size deters most would-be attackers; moreover, its thick hide is hard to pierce but predators will always seek out the young, the old, the injured, and the weak, with lions or spotted hyenas often working as a team to separate out a potential victim. A system of group defense and the mutual protectiveness of the maternal herd serve to limit opportunities for even their most persistent enemies. At night, the adults form a circle around the calves to protect them from any danger. However, if an unwise calf wanders away from the herd during the day, it may well be seized as a predator's lucky lunch break.

Above and left: When water is scarce, lions and elephants often converge at sought-after waterholes. Despite the elephant's much greater size, a pride of lions will attack an elephant that is separated from the herd, especially at night when the excellent night vision of the lions gives them a considerable advantage.

Marching ever onward

Much of an elephant's day is spent walking and eating. Elephant herds travel for many miles to seek out food and water, meandering along in single file.

Much of the time is spent grazing. In the rainy season, fodder is rarely scarce and the herds may browse for up to 22 hours each day, following a regular routine, drinking and feeding in familiar places with the large males taking their food at some distance from the main herd.

These browsing herds have a great impact on the trees and their immediate environment. It is often reported that they damage forests but, so long as their attentions are spread over a wide area and not to one confined site, this can be a force for good – or at least for change – as the elephants eventually help woodlands and savannahs mutate into grasslands. They keep the savannah clear by eating the shrubs and trees, which in turn gives the grass the opportunity to grow, allowing many other grazers to survive.

Above and right: Elephants are constantly on the move, marching and munching, needing prodigious amounts of food to fuel their great bulk. An adult consumes at least 220 to 440lb (100 to 200kg) of vegetation each day.

Migratory journeys make up the cycle of the elephant's year and the regular routes are taught to each new generation. Younger elephants have to learn the route maps from their elders, led by the matriarch as they move ever onward through the landscape, ranging through a wide tract of land in their endless search for fresh food. Elephants must always retain at least one foot on the ground so they assume an ambling walk, normally at a rate of about 4 to 5mph (6–8kph) that may rise to 6 to 8mph (10–13kph) if they take longer, quicker strides. Charging or fleeing elephants may reach 25mph (40kph) – which is much faster than humans can run.

As well as sitting on their haunches as a halfway stage to lying down or rising, elephants may assume a semi-erect position to reach fruit high up a tree, or to mount a female. When desperate to reach the mineral salts they so adore, some (particularly those without tusks) will practically stand on their heads if this proves the only way to reach the tastiest deposits. Moreover, elephants are perfectly capable of climbing up and sliding down steep slopes. Although they have learned the art of three-point turns, they will often walk backward instead as this requires less energy than turning fully around.

Whatever the stance demanded by specific situations, an elephant will cover about 15 miles (25km) per day but on occasions may walk for over 45 miles (70km). Distances as great as 125 miles (200km) per day have been recorded in the Namibian desert.

Left: *Elephants will often cover great distances looking for fresh grass and water. Finding or crossing a river or lake offers a welcome opportunity to drink and cool off, and perhaps to swim.*

Following pages: *Two young elephants set out on a journey, protected on each side by mothers with well-rounded udders. A baby will be up on its feet within 30 minutes of birth and can join the herd in a few days. Under the matriarch's guidance, the herd slows down for a while and makes frequent stops until the new young ones have developed enough stamina to keep up.*

Rest and sleep

In between all this traveling, an elephant still finds time to enjoy washing, grooming, courtship, and family contact. Large mammals need less sleep than smaller ones but the whole herd rests for a few hours in the morning and then again, when the sun is at its hottest, they will snooze in the shade.

The matriarch may lead the herd to a familiar safe retreat but elephants never drop their guard and their rest is constantly interrupted. Babies generally lie down to sleep, but researchers report that many elephants rest standing up at night and lie down only for a couple of hours before dawn. Up or down, the group never 'switch off' all at the same time and an elephant usually enjoys a maximum of four hours' snatched slumber. At least one member of the herd is almost always awake or in a semi-doze on guard duty, while the others moan in their dreams and snore loudly.

Above: While mature elephants generally doze standing up, babies and youngsters will flop down on the ground to sleep while others stand guard close by.

Right: Elephants do not sleep for long periods; that would expose them to danger but they do seek the opportunity to rest in cool shade when the sun is blazing down and the temperature peaks.

Above: *Sources of water are vital gathering places where different groups will come and go, each herd led by a matriarch. Elephants of all ages adore water and play in it even as adults.*

Right: *Because their stomachs need constant filling and because they must take it in turns to be on guard duty, elephants do not sleep for long but tend to snatch brief ten-minute naps.*

Right: A baby sleeps between the adults' great feet. Elephants walk on their toes with their soles acting as thick 'elastic' cushioning pads, which flatten out and expand with each step they take.

Following pages: Elephants are very caring mothers who protect their infants, bathe and scrub them, carry them over obstacles, and help them escape if they tumble into pits or ravines. They show them great affection, touching and caressing their babies very tenderly.

Life Cycles

Elephants grow up in the security of the herd, surrounded by many loving adults. The herd share the joy in a newborn's arrival and in the upbringing and defense of the youngest members of the herd – right through to maturity. Babies are vulnerable and there are dangers all around, but the adult elephants strive to give these future herd members the best possible chance of a healthy and safe infancy.

Family Matters

Baby elephants must be among the most appealing creatures in the world. Their curious faces, with whiskery chins and uncontrollable trunks, peep out from between the giant 'tree-trunk' legs of their elders in the herd, as they first survey the world. These precious infants encapsulate the future of the herd and are greatly loved and protected by every member of the family.

Their lives were conceived many, many months before after a brief courtship and an act of mating that lasted just a minute or so. However, this short encounter ensures the continuing cycle of life.

Fertility and courtship

Mating is not strictly seasonal but generally (like most births) it will occur during the rains. These couplings will be monopolized by the larger bulls, which are usually aged over 35 or so. Great numbers of elephants may gather together at this time – especially in areas where their range is limited by human enclosures – forming an association linked to the imminent peak of mating activity.

A female elephant's fertility cycle occupies a 15- to 16-week repeated pattern with estrus lasting some three days, during which her ovaries release from two to around 26 eggs.

Right: Dwarfed by its elders, this baby elephant finds a safe haven among a forest of legs, some of which belong to its mother.

Males also experience hormonal troughs and peaks, the latter being highly exaggerated during the *musth* – this is a periodic cycle seen in both African and Asian male elephants. During this time, when their blood testosterone levels are running very high, the bulls will exude heavy secretions from temporal glands that are active whenever they are excited or anxious, staining the cheeks below the glands' opening. They will also dribble urine and mark territory with this – and generally become extremely volatile in their behavior.

Competition between rival males may involve chasing and sparring with one another but this apparent aggression rarely leads to a real battle. Bulls in musth will continually seek opportunities to mate while the other 'normal' bulls will wisely allow them the precedence and space that they demand. Cows are clearly attracted to a bull that is in musth and he will be the first choice for any female in heat, but the musth is not an essential element to reproduction. Cows can breed successfully with a bull that is not in this heightened state but the increased sexual energy and aggression exhibited during musth means that they are far more likely to mate during this three-to-four-month period.

The female in heat makes infrasound calls (at a frequency inaudible to the human ear), proclaiming to any elephants within a radius of about 2 miles (3km) that she is in a receptive condition and to let them know her location. Obviously it is the bulls that are most likely to respond to this announcement.

Once they have found each other, the cow and bull commence their courtship. The roused male will follow and chase the female until she decides to receive his attentions. During her initial nervous, watchful behavior, she will keep moving quickly out of the way, with her eyes very wide open and her head held higher than usual. Moving away from the rest of the herd, the female keeps her tail raised, her head ever twisted around to check on her pursuing suitor. Sometimes she demonstrates this 'estrous walk' as she keeps a gleaming eye on all the male elephants that are roused and ready to mate.

Above and opposite: *The mature bull, ready to mate, will soon locate a female in heat, attracted by the infrasound calls she is making that he can detect up to 2 miles (3km) away.*

The female may circle around and return to the herd, and will cease this dodging, dancing tease only when overtaken by the bull and finally brought face to face. At last the female separates out from the herd properly and prepares to mate with her suitor. Meanwhile, any other males around will join in the excitement, milling around the courting couple – making loud calls, defecating and urinating, shaking their heads, and flapping their ears.

Initially, the pair caress each other with their trunks and intertwine these. The male will use what is called the Jacobson's or vomeronasal organ which is found on the palate on the roof of his mouth. This special gland is a chemical-sensing organ distinct from the normal olfactory sense of smell. It is shaped like a pipe with a small entrance hole that leads up to nerves in the skull. The male uses it to test out the female's reproductive status. He places his trunk inside her vulva or in her urine and then puts his trunk tip into his mouth, sipping and sniffing appreciatively. A fully receptive female seems to enjoy this stage of the pre-nuptials.

Above: After an initial session of playing 'hard to get' and dancing away, the female will allow the bull to approach her and they will caress each other with their trunks.

Right: Only the most dominant males are permitted to breed with receptive females. The less dominant ones must wait their turn. It is usually the older and larger bulls, who may be 40 to 50 years old, that do most of the breeding.

Opposite: *Elephants love to relax and play in water and so it is appropriate that courtship and mating will sometimes take place in a pool, river, or lake.*

Above: *When the female is nearly ready to mate, there is a good deal of face-to-face contact, with trunks entwining and touching, mouth caresses, and overt displays of affection.*

Mating

Preparatory maneuvers involve a good deal of mutual touching and caressing, face-to-face, mouths touching, and trunks twining. At last the receptive female will turn and brace herself ready for the male to get into position – a complicated procedure for such heavy animals.

The act of mating takes some practice and younger males are unlikely to be successful in their first attempts, especially as the females prefer the more experienced older males and are likely to reject the smaller males at the last minute.

The couple may mate several times over a period of three to four days, and sometimes they may decide to mate in the water, among the other herd members that may be cooling off there.

Above: *Females ovulate for only a few days each year. Here one signals her readiness to a mate as their trunks move in perfect harmony and, very aptly, create a heart-shaped silhouette.*

Left: *Once the receptive female has stopped evading the male, he will approach her gently and caress her tenderly with his trunk.*

Pregnancy

Figures and reference sources do vary but, however the count is taken, the elephant's gestation period is very long. It takes from 18 to 23 months (550-690 days) for the fetus to reach full term. Some experts have suggested that male infants may take slightly longer to reach full development than the females do and that the African's gestation period tends to be slightly longer than the Asian's, which averages out at only 609 days – over 20 months.

During the first three months of pregnancy, the fetus grows quickly and the newly forming ears, trunk, and tail soon appear. The expectant mother's mammary glands begin to produce milk and she may now associate closely with a mature female companion who will ultimately help her to deliver and to raise the young elephant (and who can become a quite possessive 'aunt').

Eventually, as the pregnancy advances to full term, the calf reaches its birth weight of about 200 to 220lb (90 to 100kg) for a female and some 265lb (120kg) for a male. A sudden fall in the mother elephant's progesterone levels (progesterone is a hormone that maintains pregnancy) indicates that the gestation period is drawing to a close and that birth is imminent.

Above and right: *Females have to cope with a gestation period of some 18 to 23 months – the longest in the animal kingdom – but the pregnancy will not become obvious to any human observers until the last four to six months.*

The first few hours

A mother elephant, anticipating birth, will seek a place where a sweep of grass or soft ground will make a gentle birth site for the baby. The mother usually stays up on her legs, with hind legs splayed out, as her infant emerges into the world – wrapped in the thin membrane of an embryonic sac. Another cow often assists the mother during the birth and either of this pair will break the sac open to free the infant. The birth is usually a single delivery; twins are born only very rarely (a 1.35 percent possibility). The placenta will be delivered about 30 minutes later.

Meanwhile, the newborn elephant is drawing its first breaths as it recovers from its momentous arrival into a strange new world. The baby begins to wriggle its ears, tail, and trunk and finally struggles upright onto its feet, usually within half an hour or so of its arrival, helped up by nudges from its mother's trunk and feet. In no time at all, the calf is standing up, albeit shakily, on its newly discovered legs, and it raises its tiny wobbling, and as yet uncontrollable, trunk (a baby takes some time to learn how to maneuver this clumsy long appendage) until its mouth at last discovers its mother's nipple. Then it stretches up enthusiastically to take its first feed, sucking greedily on the nourishing milk from mammary glands situated between mother's sturdy front legs. The baby uses its mouth to suckle, not its trunk, which it flips back out of the way.

The new arrival will soon arouse great interest among the rest of the herd who gather round to inspect the latest family member, showing great pleasure and excitement as they touch the youngster very gently, sniffing its new scent and making soft rumbling noises of appreciation.

Left: *Females give birth at intervals of about every five years and while the length of the labor ranges from five minutes to 60 hours, the average is about 11 hours. The mother will generally be helped by an older and more experienced female. Just like a midwife, she assists with both the birth and the baby's first moments of life.*

Above: A strong bond soon develops between the mother and calf who are constantly in close physical contact with one another.

Opposite: A newly born elephant soon discovers its mother's nipple and sucks vigorously. Just as a human baby sometimes sucks its thumb, the calf will often seek comfort by sucking its trunk.

Right: The mother guards the new arrival and guides it carefully over or around obstacles with her trunk. Here they negotiate a ditch.

Following pages: When the baby is some two days old, it will be strong enough to join the herd that has been waiting nearby, ready to introduce the new arrival to more of its surroundings.

Infancy

The new baby elephant suckles several times an hour, gaining 22 to 44lb (10–20kg) each month, and in the process developing an extremely strong bond with its mother – if this is a daughter, such close contact may endure for some 50 more years. Soon the mother begins the routine of washing her calf by gently squirting water over it and then scrubbing the little one with her trunk. If drought strikes, she will regurgitate water from her stomach and spray it over her baby to keep it cool.

This is a well-disciplined world and the young elephant quickly discovers that, however adored it might be, unacceptable behavior will quickly warrant a slap as a reprimand. There is also tender comfort to be had, however, when the mother or other members of the herd offer a reassuring touch, an embrace, or a comforting rub with a foot – whatever the occasion demands.

Above: The young elephant drinks its mother's milk little and often and will suckle for a considerable time, probably at least two years. It all depends on when she begins her next pregnancy.

Right: Mother and infant develop very close affectionate bonds that may last a lifetime if the calf is female. The young ones soon become playful and curious about the world beyond their mother's immediate proximity but still need regular reassurance from her.

Some cows may continue to provide milk throughout their childbearing years and there are instances when related cows may suckle one another's calves. During its first year, while it is still small enough to walk underneath its mother, the baby will remain constantly beside or beneath her. She will protect her infant from danger or offer shade from the hot sun by pushing it safely under her shadow. Much tender care is lavished on the baby by all the adults, who skillfully avoid stepping on this tiny creature frolicking at their feet. A young elephant may continue to nurse well into its third or fourth year, still staying close to mother, marching along with the herd guided by a firm grip on her tail – or steered from behind as the adult seizes the younger one's tail. Meanwhile, mother helps the youngster in more difficult terrain, lifting it up over awkward obstacles, crooking her trunk around its rump to help it scramble up a steep slope or rescuing it from a too-deep muddy wallow.

The mother's rich milk frees her offspring from the chore of grazing vegetation for hours on end and so allows plenty of time for play while the adults feed. Gradually, the youngster begins to explore farther afield, running back to mother for security whenever the situation proves uncomfortable. A squeal of distress will immediately summon help or protection from both mother and other herd members. By the time it is five years old, the infant will be playing happily with other young elephants, learning how to find food and how to associate with the rest of the herd while not straying more than a few yards away from its mother. It will remain dependent on her for eight to ten years, being quickly retrieved if it should stray more than a few yards away.

Above: Rough and tumble is all part of the fun of being an infant and the males often play more roughly than females.

Below: Before long the energetic youngsters gain confidence and begin to venture a little farther away from their mothers.

Opposite: Young elephants have a long period of learning stretching ahead of them and mastering how to use the trunk is just one of the things to be conquered.

Following pages: A young elephant's dependency on its elders lasts almost as long as a human's. An orphan of under two years is very unlikely to survive; 70 percent of orphans aged from two to five will share a similar fate; and half of those who lose their mothers while only five to ten years old will die.

Above: An African baby elephant has to stretch up farther to reach the nipple than does an Asian one, whose mother has shorter legs.

Above: A mother constantly checks on her youngster and so even when he is walking in her wake, she keeps in touch with him using her hind foot and the odd swish of her tail.

Left: A new baby is given a very warm, excited reception by the rest of the herd who touch it gently, sniff it, and rumble and roar their appreciation. The herd, especially sisters and aunts, will continue to provide the infant with much love, care, and attention.

Growing up

A young cow reaches puberty sometime after the age of ten or 11 and may well become pregnant very quickly afterward. So it is possible for her to produce her first calf when she is aged only about 12, 13, or 14. Gradually, ties to the herd, rather than just her mother, lead to greater independence as the young female becomes fully socialized into the matriarchal network. By the time she is 15 she will almost certainly have given birth to a single baby, although elephants are not considered to be fully mature adults until they are aged about 20.

Theoretically, a young female will proceed to give birth every four or five years, but a nine-year gap is not uncommon. She will remain fertile up until she reaches her 60s. However, many factors can interrupt the production line, including the kind of stress invoked by human interference, mass tourism, overcrowded conditions, or by drought when conception is naturally inhibited and a lower reproductive rate prevails.

Meanwhile, a young bull is able to produce sperm from the age of ten to 15 years. By the time he is 25 or so, he will begin competing for females.

Right: Young elephants practice trunk grappling and tasting, using this flexible tentacle-like appendage to play and to communicate, and so developing complex social and communication skills they will need to use in later adult life.

Following pages: Two young elephants stand mouth-to-mouth, sharing close physical contact. Calves learn their behavior largely by observing and copying adults, not by instinct alone.

Above: *Trunk contact between two youngsters: the elephant's finger-like trunk tip is able to cope with very delicate manipulation and as the youngsters gain better control they will be able to touch, tease, and grasp the tiniest objects.*

Right: *Like humans, each half of an elephant's brain principally controls the opposite half of its body. The dextrous use of its very versatile trunk requires a lot of elephant brainpower and the favored side for the trunk can be the elephant equivalent of being left- or right-handed.*

Following pages: *A young elephant grows up surrounded by a caring family and related cows may suckle one another's calves. From an early age the infants will be marching along with the herd, guided by a firm grip on their mothers' tails — or steered from behind.*

In their prime

Most of an elephant's physical bulk will have been attained by the time the animal is 20 years old but a small degree of growth continues throughout its life. An elephant reaches its full mental capacity when aged between 30 and 45.

Although adult bulls remain largely solitary, at times they gather in bachelor groups and, even when seemingly apart, they remain continually in contact with other nearby elephants through both scent messages and infrasonic (low-frequency) signals. Young bulls soon discover and respect the capabilities of other bulls in their vicinity and the males establish a hierarchy. As they age and grow, they will compete in the breeding arena and, generally, the older an elephant bull, the more successful he will be there.

Adult elephants continue to revel in close physical contact; family members will stand touching one another while resting or drinking. They lean and rub their bodies together, often touching one another with their trunks. Both African and Asiatic males may explore same-sex bonding accompanied by affectionate caressing, or they place their trunks in each other's mouths or intertwine them. Living as they do in mosty single-sex communities, both sexes form strong, long-lasting relationships with other individuals of the same gender.

Right: Young bulls leave their family herd at puberty and seek the company of other young bulls, learning more about adult life from high-ranking males. Young bulls greatly respect these dominant males and can develop for them a kind of 'hero-worship.'

Above: *A solitary male flaps his ears. Young bulls often gather together to form bachelor herds but an adult in his prime will generally live alone, albeit while remaining in touch using the various methods that elephants employ to communicate.*

Left: *It is the matriarch and the older females who keep the bull calves in line during their infancy and youth. However, once their mid-teens arrive, it is time for the males to leave and find their feet in a bachelor society where they will complete the process of growing up.*

Following pages: *The adult male is a mighty, impressive animal with strong tusks that are used for battle and self-defense, to dig up roots and water, scrape and gouge out minerals, and sometimes even as a form of pickax.*

Senior citizens and death

Elephants can live to 60 or 70 years old, death usually being heralded by the wearing out of the last set of teeth. If the old elephant that has died is one of the herd, rather than a solitary beast, the family members will stay by the corpse for a long while. They appear to undergo an intense mourning period, sometimes conducting week-long vigils over the body, and then participating in a burial ritual, carefully covering the corpse with earth and brush.

Sometimes, the elephants may revisit the site for years afterward, caressing the bones with their trunks and even taking turns to rub their trunks along the teeth in the lower jaw of the skull, just as living elephants do when they greet each other.

When a matriarch dies, this is a time of especially deep mourning as the herd members touch her body and fondle her bones in a strange, silent vigil, seeming to need physical contact and returning many times to the body. Even if the elephant is a stranger whose bones are discovered on the herd's travels, the elephants will still pause, fondle the bones, and seem to grieve.

Of course young elephants may die too: hunters – human or animal – may kill an elephant in its prime or seize a youngster. A baby may be stillborn and then its mother will often maintain an inconsolable vigil over the corpse for at least three days. Whatever the circumstances, the other elephants' grief is evident and very moving for those who have observed this phenomenon. If harm comes to any member of an elephant group, all the other elephants are immediately aware of it – and this strong cohesion is especially evident in the event of a death.

Opposite and right: Elephants may reach a good age – sometimes they live to be 60 or 70 years old. During this time each of their molar teeth will have been replaced four times. When an elephant's last tooth is gone, starvation and death will be inevitable.

Are there any elephant graveyards?

Many legends and romantic anecdotes suggest that elephants slip away to secret communal places to die among the remains of their forefathers. Undoubtedly large piles of elephant bones are found in certain places and this probably inspired stories of elephant graveyards. However, it is likely that these accumulations of bones are, in fact, places where mass deaths occurred – such as dangerous river crossings or bogs that claimed elephant lives.

Most probably, such bone sites were former watering holes where large numbers of elephants may have gathered in times of great drought. Desperately seeking to drink and cool their bodies, the many thirsty elephants may ultimately

have perished together as the mud baked unmercifully and finally became their communal grave.

Thus we have gone full circle following the events that mark the milestones of an elephant's life. While birth is obviously an occasion full of joy for all the herd, the elephants' mourning for the loss of a beloved herd member demonstrates equally strongly their great sensitivity and emotional response to all matters that form part of their family life.

Above and opposite: *When a herd member dies, elephants grieve; they mourn lost friends. They shed tears when they are afraid or experiencing sorrow – and clearly feel deep emotions.*

Elephants and People

While human-elephant **contact** has often been disfigured by the **ravages** of hunters, **poachers**, and **ivory** traders, there are more **positive** experiences too. Elephants have carried **princes**, been dressed in finery for **processions**, depicted in **art**, literature, and myth, **worshiped** – and photographed on many a **safari**. Respect and **love** for this **amazing** animal has contributed enormously to the life **experience** of many people, bringing **pleasure** and fulfillment. The **ultimate** experience, however, is to see them **roaming free**.

The Influence of Humans

The elephant has long been associated with the lives and cultures of human beings: sometimes this has been through a clear physical interaction as men and women meet elephants in the jungle or grassland, hunt them for their meat or ivory, observe or photograph them, tame them to be used as working beasts, or exploit them in the zoo and circus. Other times, in counterpoint to this *real* physical contact, elephants have been absorbed into our dreams and imaginings, depicted in art and literature, described in legend and myth, or revered as religious beings – gods even. Their size has made them perpetual symbols of strength while their longevity has added to their status.

The working elephant

The working elephant is not a new concept. Humans may well have tamed elephants over 3000 years ago. There are carved images that may portray domesticated elephants on seals from the Indus Valley that possibly date from as long ago as 1500 BC.

Certainly, the Asian elephant, in particular, has been a beast of burden and a working partner of mankind for centuries. This great animal, with its ability to march for many miles, is the ultimate 'off-road vehicle' and can keep a firm foothold even in the worst conditions when monsoons have turned tracks into lethal mud slides. The elephant can stride out – confident that its huge heel pads will grip the ground securely, whatever the conditions.

Right: Warriors and finely-dressed elephants are here depicted on a bas-relief wall panel thought to date back to the early 1200s at the Bayon temple in Angkor Thom, Cambodia.

In the remotest areas, such as parts of South-East Asia, it is often more economical to use elephants for heavy work than to attempt to transport and manipulate modern machinery. None the less, a working elephant does need 300 to 600lb (135–270kg) of food each day to fuel its labors. But while it has been trained, the elephant has never truly been domesticated or subjected to selective breeding to 'improve' its usefulness to mankind, as has happened with other animals such as dogs, cattle, and horses.

Training an African elephant

Although African elephants are deemed more challenging to discipline than Asian elephants because of their more sensitive temperaments, some sources claim that they are actually easier to train – provided appropriate methods are used (which may be different to the ones used for their Asian cousins). They must also be trained from infancy. African elephants have worked for humans, mostly during wartime. It is known that some, if not all, of the elephants that carried Hannibal's troops across the Alps to attack the Romans in 218 BC were African, probably the slightly smaller forest variety.

Rather more recently (in colonial times) African forest elephants have been used to work in the Belgian Congo (now the Democratic Republic of Congo). Experienced Indian mahouts (riders of elephants) were brought in to catch and train the African elephants, in this case using the Asian method – but only with young orphans. Some tamed African elephants are now ridden on photographic safari tours, while others haul logs.

The different attitudes toward elephants that are apparent in Africa and Asia are of ancient origin and they remain deeply entrenched. As long ago as 300 BC there was a taboo on killing elephants in India's Mauryan Empire because elephants were needed for the king's army and he also insisted that the forests should be preserved as their habitat. This conservation debate continues in Asia today.

In Africa, however, the elephant is not, and never has been, revered in the same way. In 2003, Professor Raman Sukumar speaking at Oxford University suggested that the culture of capturing and taming elephants died out in Africa but survived in Asia because there it coincided with the rise of strong republics and kingdoms for which elephants . . . 'are, and have been, more useful to locals alive than dead whereas in Africa, they can be more useful to locals dead than alive.' Certainly working elephants have been used in Asia over the centuries in armies and in industries like logging and construction, whereas in Africa they have faced slaughter and poaching for ivory and so their relationship with people has generally been a harsher and more bitter experience.

Above: Today tourists in Africa not only hope to catch a glimpse of elephants in the wild but may also venture out riding on African elephants, defying the long-held belief that these are not so readily trained as their Asian counterparts.

Opposite: Mahouts develop very close relationships with their Asian elephant charges and, under their guidance, the elephants will help in many forestry tasks, contributing to the felling of trees, carrying smaller logs in their trunks, and hauling enormous weights.

Following pages: Mahouts bathe their elephants at the renowned Elephant Nature Park near Chiang Mai, Thailand. Established as a sanctuary for distressed elephants in 1996 by Sangduen 'Lek' Chailert who was appalled at the conditions in which many working elephants were kept, guest volunteers have the opportunity for close contact with the animals as they help with the care of the 25 to 30 elephants kept here.

Forestry and logging

During peaceful times the ancient kings of Sri Lanka used elephants to help in the construction of their cities. Elephants would haul the heaviest building materials, such as mighty granite columns, pulling heavily loaded lowbed carts. Some societies even employed elephants as executioners to crush convicted culprits underfoot!

Today humans still use elephants for forestry tasks that require great strength – like hauling logs or uprooting trees and moving tree trunks. Although replaced by modern tractors in many places, elephants are often regarded as the better option because they do less damage to the forest ecosystem, especially in precious rainforests.

Once upon a time elephants were also employed in timber operations in the lush teak forests that flourished in places like Thailand. Sadly, most of these South-East Asian forests where elephants once worked – especially in Cambodia, Sumatra, and Thailand – are disappearing at an alarming rate, because of illegal logging operations and slash-and-burn agriculture practices. In fact, Thailand has now been forced to ban legal logging (since 1990). Now thousands of mahouts (elephant keepers and caretakers) find themselves unemployed while many working elephants have been neglected or misused as a result of the decline in this industry. Meanwhile, the habitat continues to disappear, although ironically illegal logging practices may still employ several thousand elephants.

It is generally more economical to capture wild young elephants and tame them for work in the forests than to attempt to breed them in captivity, where births are rare. Until recently, a trained elephant would be used to help calm a freshly captured elephant in a corral until it could be securely tethered but today tranquillizing dart guns are used to subdue the frightened newcomer.

234   Elephants and People

Meanwhile, the mahouts usually develop very close relationships with their charges and under their guidance elephants will help to fell trees selectively, to carry smaller logs in their trunks, and to haul enormous weights (over four tons) of logs – sometimes as a pair harnessed together. The ancient traditions of the working elephant survive in Myanmar – but in rapidly vanishing forests.

Above and opposite: *Here in the forests of Myanmar a Burmese mahout directs an Asian elephant as it grapples with a heavy teak log (above) and (opposite) an elephant hauls a heavy log burden up a steep muddy incline.*

Elephants go to war

Elephants have sometimes been described as the forerunners of the military tank and male elephants have long been used by humans in campaigns of war. They went into battle with the Persians and, after Alexander's victory over the Indian king Porus at the battle of the Hydaspes in 326 BC, captured war elephants became a symbol of imperial power and were depicted as an emblem on coins. Their immense size and strength lent campaigners several advantages – not least one of surprise, as in the case of Hannibal, renowned for his use of elephants.

Hannibal Barca, one of the finest war commanders in history, exploited elephants for military purposes. A young general from the city of Carthage in what is now Tunisia in North Africa, he spearheaded an attack against the Romans in Italy in 218 BC, approaching from Spain and leading an army of 40,000 soldiers and 38 elephants through Spain and into France. After crossing the River Rhone with the elephants transported on massive rafts, he crossed the Alps into Italy and proceeded to win several battles on his march south – but he failed to seize Rome. It was probably North African forest elephants that went to war under his command. While slightly smaller than their savannah cousins, these were certainly large enough to cause tremendous damage to infantry and to terrify the opponents – and their cavalry horses – when they charged toward them.

Soon the Romans absorbed this clever tactic into their own culture and it is thought that Julius Caesar traveled on an elephant during his 54 BC invasion of Britain, riding in a high 'howdah' that resembled a castle. The sight of this enormous strange beast, the first of its type seen on British soil since the disappearance of the mammoths, caused huge consternation and panic. The Britons fled, thus allowing the Romans to proceed across the River Thames unopposed.

In 1398, the great Timur, King of Samarkand, attacked Delhi and found that the city was defended by an elephant corps but the animals stampeded when Timur's soldiers drove torch-carrying camels toward them.

The Burmese developed an ingenious type of elephant-top fortification from which about a dozen warriors could shoot arrows, throw javelins, or wield long spears. In the 1600s, there are records of an elephant in India that was provided with a suit of armor made of chain-mail and overlapping metal plates.

Elephants have remained an important form of military transport and reconnaissance aid in difficult jungle terrain, able to push their way through thick vegetation, cross fast-flowing water and climb steep slopes. They have several advantages over conventional vehicles – they provide a convenient high viewpoint, need just the immediate vegetation as fuel, are able to ford rivers, leave no tire tracks and move far more quietly than a motorized truck.

In Sri Lanka, the elephant was used as a personnel carrier in many wars fought against invading forces. During World War II, elephants helped to haul Allied aircraft during the Far East campaigns, carried heavy military equipment in the mud and up the steep slopes of the Asian theaters of war, and were also involved in the building of the infamous bridge over the River Kwai in Siam (now Thailand).

Even as recently as the 1960s, elephants were implemented to transport military supplies to the forces during the Vietnam War.

Above left: *Elaborately decorated elephants and their mahouts wait at the Amber Fort in Rajasthan, ready to take tourists for a ride during which they can enjoy an elevated view of the area's attractions, in particular the fine marble and red sandstone fort built in 1592.*

Opposite: *This battle scene depicted in a 17th-century Mughal miniature painting shows an elephant at the heart of the battle and providing his riders with the advantage of extra height.*

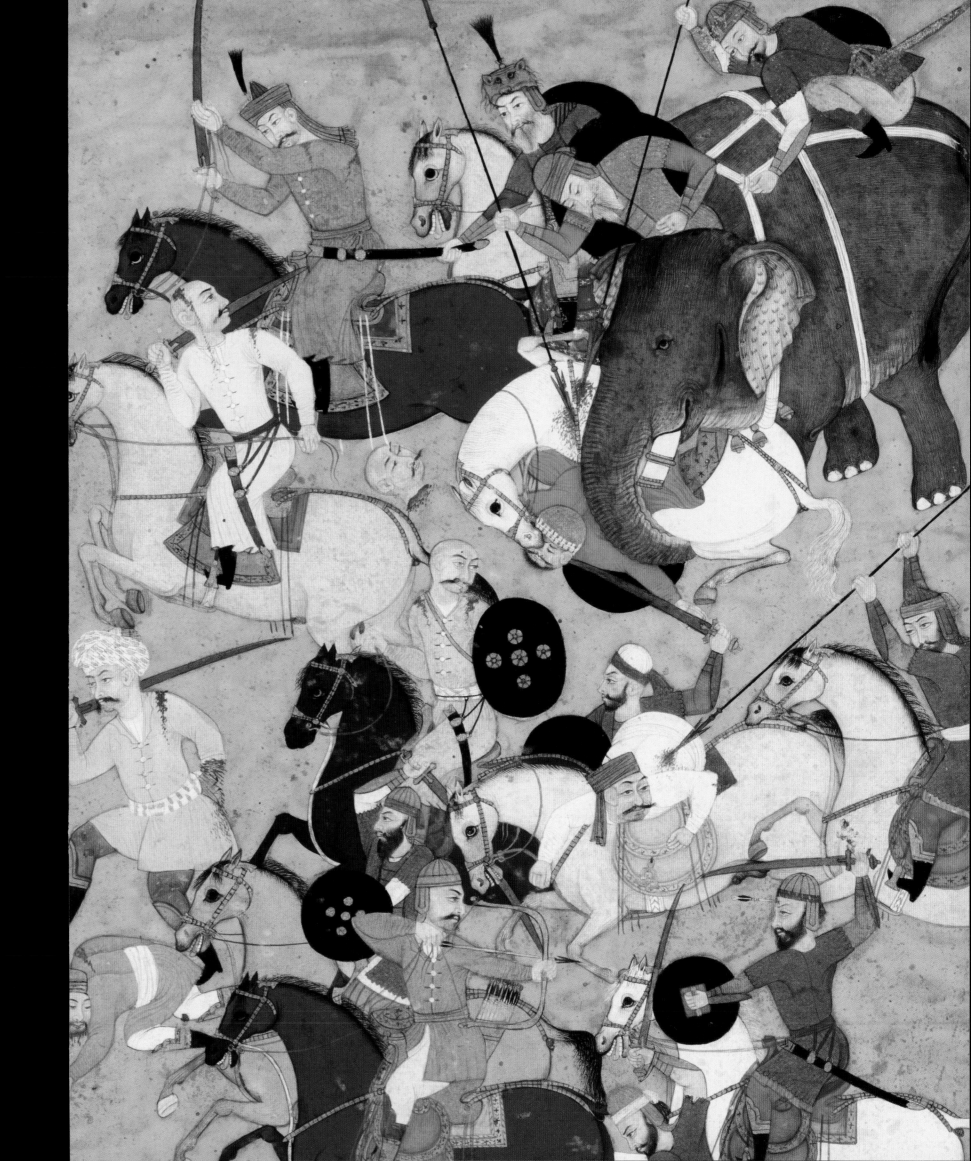

Safaris and hunting

Once the Europeans had begun to explore the interior of Asia, in particular during Britain's imperial domination of India, the image of the Victorian hunter (often an army officer or an aristocrat), in sola topi helmet and sporting a rifle atop an elephant, became an archetype. This practice is one factor that has contributed to the near-demise of the tiger as a viable species, for these magnificent beasts were often the object of the hunt and many a tiger skin was sent back to Europe as a trophy after a hunting expedition involving the use of elephants. The local populations had, of course, used elephants on hunting trips for tigers and boar long before the Europeans arrived.

The elephant is an ideal means of transport, providing prince, officer, or explorer with an excellent and relatively safe vantage point from which to view – and sadly also to shoot – the wildlife of Asia. The mobile viewing platform proved ideal as it raised the travelers high above the tall grass – and it still serves this purpose for 21st century tourists with rather less aggressive tendencies, shooting with cameras now, rather than guns.

Today, scientific researchers use elephants as transportation too, so that they can penetrate and study wildlife in swampy areas that would otherwise be inaccessible and with less risk of their human interventions frightening away their quarry. They penetrate the jungle unobtrusively and are far quieter than motor transport.

Above: *An elephant crosses a river in the tropical jungles of Sri Lanka, as its tourist passengers scan the surroundings for interesting wildlife – birds and butterflies, monitor lizards, sambar deer, and monkeys.*

Opposite: *African elephants take tourists on safari in Zimbabwe, Africa. Riding so high provides a wonderful view of the bush terrain and the wild animals. The elephant carers here are called indunas.*

Poaching and ivory

Because elephants are so large, they have no significant natural enemies except for people, who have slaughtered elephants for their ivory tusks since time immemorial. Trying to curtail the illegal ivory trade proves a constant challenge as this 'white gold' fetches such a high price. Scientists are now using DNA fingerprinting to trace the original location of stolen tusks.

In recent years, with diminishing numbers of elephants, the impact of poaching reached crisis point and, in 1989, a group of 115 countries together formed the United Nations 'Convention on International Trade in Endangered Species' (or CITES). The international sale of ivory was banned and, fortunately, the scale of elephant hunting has now diminished, but complacency is not an option. Elephants are still slaughtered to fuel the continued greed for ivory and some reports suggest that poaching may be on the increase again. The sight of a great pile of seized ivory is an appalling reminder of the vast scale of the killings.

Many elephants are slain for meat too, and this remains a serious threat to their welfare, especially in Central Africa where illegal killing is widespread. Meanwhile, unscrupulous animal suppliers continue to seize elephants, removing them indiscriminately from their homelands and their families for commercial gain.

In 1989, after the African elephant population had dropped from several million to fewer than 700,000 in just nine decades, and halving during just the 1980s, hunting of the African elephant and ivory trading were forbidden.

Above: *Over 20 tons of elephant tusks, seized from poachers, burn like a funeral pyre – this is one haul that will never be sold.*

Uneasy neighbors

Human populations in Africa and Asia have quadrupled since the turn of the century – the fastest rate on the planet – and so the relationship between elephant and human populations has become increasingly uncomfortable. They are direct competitors for living space as more people than ever need timber for fuel and housing and land to grow crops. As a consequence forest and savannah are being turned into cropland and livestock pasture.

These farmers and families do not regard elephants as good neighbors, especially when they damage fences and raid crops. The elephants, however, seem oblivious to the anger they arouse as they find, for example, delicious pineapple seemingly laid out in neat rows ready for them to eat. The furious farmers, however, may poison or shoot these intruders on their land to protect their crops.

This uneasy relationship worsens when rogue elephants (aggressive male elephants during the breeding season) rampage through villages. Some countries have established culling programs whereby park officials or hunters are allowed to kill a predetermined number of elephants in order to keep herds manageable and minimize human-elephant confrontations.

In Asia too, elephants arouse anger when they destroy crops and pose a danger to human populations – up to 500 people every year are killed by them. Because the females have no tusks, there is less poaching here, but loss of habitat is a far greater threat to their survival.

Above: The avaricious international marketplace for ivory makes the African elephant vulnerable to very persistent poachers. Meanwhile farmers resent the elephants' destruction of crops and fencing.

Circuses and zoos

Elephants have appeared in the showring since the term circus was coined by the ancient Romans. Generally it was the (relatively) more placid and predictable female elephants that were trained to perform in the ring but Jumbo, the famous elephant owned by P.T. Barnum (of the Ringling Brothers and Barnum & Bailey Circus) in the United States was a male.

This baby elephant had been captured in Africa in 1861, taken to Cairo, sold to a Paris zoo, and was then swapped for a rhino from London Zoo. It was renamed Jumbo (after jambo or jumbe, an African word for elephant) and eventually carried thousands of children for rides at London Zoo before being bought by impresario Barnum and presented at The Greatest Show on Earth in the USA. In 1885, Jumbo was killed by a train while crossing railroad tracks in Ontario, Canada, but the term jumbo has lived on, being absorbed into the English language and used ever since to mean something huge.

It has recently been discovered that, in the years between the American Civil War and World War I, all male elephants in American circuses were slaughtered because of their uncontrollable behavior during *musth*. Gradually, only female elephants (albeit some now sporting male names) marched in the circus parade.

Meanwhile, many zoos still take pride in their elephant enclosures where these vast animals are greatly admired by the visiting public. While it is obviously preferable for these magnificent creatures to roam free, at least today's enclosures for the animals are much larger and more naturalistic than hitherto and there is a greater understanding of the elephant's needs with far more emphasis placed on educating the visitors. Baby elephants born in captivity are always greeted with delight by zookeepers and public alike and their presence is growing as artificial insemination has greatly increased their numbers. None the less, some zoos, concerned about the future welfare of elephants, have decided that it is unethical to continue displaying them to the public.

Above left: P.T. Barnum's famous elephant, Jumbo, was captured in Africa in 1861, taken to Cairo, sold to a Paris zoo and came to London Zoo (as shown here), before joining the circus.

Above: Elephants perform at the 27th Monte Carlo Circus Festival in 2002. Despite changing attitudes, elephants still star in many such shows. In 2007, one tame female escaped from an Indian circus with a wild bull elephant that broke open a gate and led her off into the jungle!

Above right: A young elephant performs tricks in Thailand: nearby Ayutthaya Elephant Camp provides homes for elephants that previously worked on Bangkok's streets.

Right: This calf was born in Berlin's Friedrichsfelde Zoo in May 2007. Initially his inexperienced mother appeared to reject him and pushed him into the moat. He was rescued by keepers and reunited with her as she settled into parenthood.

Religion and culture

A good deal is now known about the intelligence of elephants, their close family ties, ways of communication, and sensitivity. These attributes, combined with their great size and dignity, have inevitably inspired human admiration throughout the centuries and, in some places, led to their becoming part of the spiritual culture.

The elephant has many associations in Asian culture. In Thailand, for example, the elephant is the national symbol and has been depicted on buildings and in statues. Between 1816 and 1916 an image of the elephant appeared on Thailand's national flag.

The elephant is often regarded as having mystical powers or as being the bearer of a prophet or god. In some instances, it is even worshiped as a god itself. The elephant's sacred standing in India, where a vast proportion of the people are Hindus, often protects it from being killed. Some temple elephants even give blessings.

Above: At the World Heritage site of Mamallapuram in India, these wonderful gigantic relief sculptures of elephants date from the 600s.

Below: A Hindu woman receives a gentle blessing from a regal, bejeweled, beautifully decorated and manicured elephant at a temple in Kanchipuram, India – one of the holy places of Shakti worship.

Ganesh

The Hindu god, Ganesh or Ganesha, is the god of teachers and students, a bringer of good fortune, the remover of obstacles who will help, if asked, those setting out on a journey, buying a vehicle, or facing testing times, such as examinations or launching a new enterprise. He is also the god of art, science, letters, and writing.

Ganesh has the head of an elephant, which symbolizes wisdom and knowledge. His large ears symbolize the patience to listen and his small eyes can see the future and perceive truth. His long trunk sniffs out good and evil while his enormous belly shows that he can digest the best – and the worst – in life.

His coloring is usually red or orange and he generally has four arms, and sometimes three eyes. Ganesha carries a bead and certain other items like a lotus flower while he sits with a bowl of sweetmeats before him. A mouse or rat will be around him – he often uses a mouse or a rat as his mount.

Above: In Mumbai, India, at the festival of the elephant-headed Ganesh, gigantic statues of this god of wisdom and success are taken in grand procession and then immersed in the sea.

Below: Elephants and pilgrims in the pink glow of dawn: both festivals and religious occasions in India often involve elephants.

Festivals and ceremonies

Elephants have long been used in ceremonies and to impress the onlooker. In ancient Rome, they took part in military pageants and performed in amphitheaters but it is in Asia that the elephant has played the greatest role in religion and ceremony. Their important cultural significance is reflected by their use in many festivals, when they will be dressed in great finery.

Buddhist temples often choose a fine elephant to carry precious relics in procession. The ornately decorated animal walks majestically through the streets. In the annual ceremony at Kandy in Sri Lanka, it is considered to be the only creature with sufficient grace to carry the sacred reliquary containing the precious tooth-relic of the Buddha.

Sometimes, such as at the elephant festival in Rajasthan, India, the skins of the elephants that take part in the parade are painted with incredible patterns and swirls of color; even their toenails may be colored. Wearing rich fabric drapings and glittering ornaments, the brilliantly decorated elephants create an amazing spectacle as they process through the streets – amid music, dancing, and swirls of confetti.

Elephant statues and models are often kept in people's homes as symbols of good luck and every year at the end of India's ten-day festival celebrating the birth of Ganesh, countless clay statues of the elephant-headed god – some huge models that arrive on trucks or carts – are tossed into the rivers or seas.

Above: The Holi Festival of Colors and annual Elephant Festival in Jaipur, India, celebrates spring's arrival with bonfires, dancing and parades of elephants, adorned with jingling trinkets. The mahouts paint the elephants' trunks, foreheads, and feet with floral motifs.

Above left: Attracting teams from all over the world, the King's Cup Elephant Polo Tournament is a charitable event held in Thailand to raise funds for the country's National Elephant Institute in Lampang. The Institute provides medical care, sustenance, employment, welfare and mahout training to Thailand's elephant population.

Opposite: Here at the Festival of Colors near Jaipur, in Rajasthan, a vividly painted elephant is groomed to perfection, painted in intricate detail, and draped in rich scarves and tassels.

Myths, legends and art

It is said that elephants never forget. Certainly they show amazing powers of memory regarding where to go to find food and water – following the same paths for many generations. The wise matriarch, in particular, seems to recognize familiar faces, even when she has been separated from them for decades, and can discern the intent of strange elephants, whether friendly or otherwise, as well as remembering human individuals.

There are many fascinating myths and legends about elephants. Indeed, some of the very first paintings by Stone Age hunters depicted the mammoth. One Indian folktale tells how, once upon a time, elephants flew in the sky until the noise they made in a tree above him annoyed a hermit, who was especially angered when a branch broke away and hit him. So the hermit used his special powers to remove their wings. Perhaps, after all, Walt Disney's *Dumbo* was not the first elephant to fly!

In Chinese, the phrase 'to ride an elephant' sounds the same as the word for happiness. Meanwhile, Kautiliya, who was an early scholar of Buddhism in India, commented that, 'A king who always cares for the elephants like his own sons is always victorious and will enjoy the friendship of the celestial world after death.'

Above: *Detail of a carving of elephants on a royal cenotaph at the ancient garden of Kshar Bagh, Bundi, in India, and* (**right**) *superbly colored frescoes on the walls at Mandawa, Rajasthan, India.*

Spirit of the elephant

Not only are elephants amazing animals by virtue of their size and magnificent bearing but we are now beginning to realize ever more clearly that they are also highly intelligent. They develop strong family bonds and a vigorous social structure but also nurture one-to-one relationships that go far beyond the boundaries of the immediate herd, so that individuals may separate and reunite after a long period of time.

They can mimic sounds, remember the calls of a large number of other elephants and communicate in ways that we are only just beginning to appreciate. Messages sent as vibrations made by their feet transmit across long distances as low-range sound waves. Until recently it was believed that the adult males were essentially solitary creatures but now it is believed that, although living physically apart, they may nevertheless communicate with one another over considerable distances.

Moreover, these are clearly animals with long memories, which express strong emotions, and reveal much shared affection. They revel in close physical contact as they touch each other and entwine their trunks. They respond very emotionally both to the arrival of a newborn infant and to the death of a companion.

Recent research suggests that elephants have a wider range of cognitive capabilities than realized previously. Their understanding and sensitivity will only be fully appreciated if we can, in turn, apply greater understanding and sensitivity to our associations with them and pursue an open-minded

research into the lives of these amazing animals, and fight far more strongly on their behalf. It is of paramount importance that international support is given to all the national parks, together with the vital conservation and relocation programs that are working so hard to enable the elephant and its way of life to survive.

The more we understand about the elephant, the greater seems the urgency to stop further poaching and slaughter, to

make constructive efforts on the elephant's behalf, to establish wildlife corridors and monitor the status and numbers of these wonderful animals more closely. It is our responsibility to work together to save the elephant from extinction and to ensure that this awe-inspiring giant of the animal kingdom will still be here to amaze future generations, that our grandchildren will see live elephants, that they do not vanish like those other giants, the dinosaurs.

Above: *All creatures are born with innate instincts but, like humans, elephants have an enormous capacity to learn too. They develop understanding through accumulated experiences of their own and the education they receive from the herd.*

Opposite: *Elephants draw upon the herd's reservoir of memory and after 20 years of growing up, they are ready to pass their own valuable knowledge on to the younger members of the family.*

Fascinating Elephant Facts

- There are some 400,000 to 660,000 African elephants in the wild; Asian elephants are thought to number no more than 50,000 although the World Wildlife Fund suggests the figure may be only 25,600–32,750 (with 15,000 in captivity) so they are far more endangered.

- The elephant is the largest land animal in the world, with the biggest African savannah bulls measuring about 11 to 12ft (3.3 to 3.7m) high at the shoulder – and weighing up to about 10 tons. Only the giraffe is taller.

- In 1955, a gigantic elephant shot near the river Cuando, South Africa, apparently measured 13ft 2in (4m) at the shoulder, weighed 15 tons, and had tusks over 14ft (4m) long.

- The average lifespan of an elephant is about 60 to 70 years.

- Some herds may cover nearly 120 miles (200km) in a single day. Usually an elephant walks at about 4mph (6.5kph).

- Elephants use mud as a sun-barrier to protect their sensitive skins.

- An elephant's skin can be up to 1in (2.5cm) thick in some places but it is also very sensitive and can detect a fly landing on it.

- If the outside temperature rises above 77°F (25°C), the elephant fans its great ears; these are its 'air conditioners.' The blood flows through the vast network of capillaries and veins in the ears causing its temperature to drop by at least 9°F (5°C) or even more. Then it flows back to the elephant's main circulation system.

- Each elephant's ear is unique and so may be used by researchers to identify individuals. The ears of the African elephant are about three times the size of those of the Asian elephant and measure about 6ft by 4ft (1.8 by 1.2m) in area.

- The trunk has no bones but does have 16 main muscles and around 150,000 special 'muscle units' to provide fine movement, and a sensitive tip covered with nerve endings.

- The trunk is the longest animal snout in the world and is powerful enough to kill a lion with a blow. It also serves as a useful snorkel when the elephant is swimming in deep water.

- The elephant has the biggest teeth of any animal and will have six sets during its lifetime. New teeth form at the rear of the mouth, pushing older teeth farther forward until these reach the front, wear down with use, and eventually drop out.

- Its tusks are enlarged incisor teeth that are permanent and grow continuously – in the case of an adult male, nearly 7in (17cm) each year to measure almost 6ft (2m), with about a quarter of this length hidden inside the jaw. These enormous shovels – that can also rip, scrape, and serve as a weapon – weigh over 220lb (100kg) each. Elephants are right- or left-tusked, just as we are right- or left-handed.

- Elephant ivory, sometimes called 'white gold,' was turned into pool and billiard balls, as well as being intricately carved to decorate countless pieces of furniture and create objets d'art.

- The elephant has the longest gestation period of any mammal – at up to 608 days, or just over 20 months.

- Elephant milk is very rich in nutritional value – too rich, in fact, for any other animal (including humans) to digest it properly.

- Elephants remember one another, even after spending many years apart.

- When an elephant drinks, it sucks the water only part of the way up its trunk, before tilting its head up, and letting the water flow into its mouth. A refreshing elephant drink usually consists of some 2.4 gallons (9 liters) of water.

- Each elephant consumes about 550lb (250kg) of food and then deposits about 220lb (100kg) of dung a day. It also passes 530 gallons (2000 liters) of methane gas in the form of belches and flatulence.

• Elephant dung is full of grainy fibrous material. Once processed, this can make excellent paper. Those involved in the creation of this unusual product collect naturally dried elephant dung from conservation zones and take it to paper-making factories. Here it is rinsed, boiled, colored, and supplemented with extra fibers from banana trees and pineapples to make it stronger. It is then turned into small 'wafers,' spread over mesh-bottomed trays and dried in the sun before being peeled off as paper sheets.

• An elephant is surprisingly agile – it can walk forward and backward, stand on its hind legs if leaning on a tree (or another elephant if mating), clamber up steep terrain, and swim well even in deep, rushing water.

• Researchers now believe that an elephant can run at about 15mph (24kph), gaining speed by crouching and swaying as it hurries along. A charging elephant can reach speeds of over 25mph (40kph).

• Elephants can communicate over long distances, using low-frequency infrasound. Messages may, for example, warn them of impending danger or alert them that a female is on heat.

• In the early morning or evening, when the air is cool at ground level and there is little interference, the elephant's infrasonic sounds may be heard across an area of 110sq miles (285km^2).

• Fossil records indicate that the small rodent-like hyrax and larger water-dwelling dugong are both close relatives of the elephant.

• The first World War II bomb that the Allies dropped on Berlin killed the only elephant in the zoo there.

• Aristotle, the ancient Chinese and the early Christians all praised the elephant's chastity, faithfulness, and modesty. It was believed to mate only very rarely – and only in water which it does, in fact, do occasionally.

• In Siam (Thailand), the emperor was called Lord of the White Elephant. The rare white elephant is considered a gift from the gods in this country – and Buddha chose an albino elephant as one of his incarnations.

• Some Siamese emperors would give white elephants to courtiers who offended them. Forbidden to ride, work, or kill these animals, the offenders, none the less, still had the great expense of caring for them. This is the origin of the term 'white elephant' for a useless possession.

• Some Asian cultures believe that elephants bring good luck and wisdom; they symbolize strength of mind in Buddhism, embodying the boundless powers and strength of the Buddha.

• The ancient Roman authors Pliny and Aelian asserted that elephants worshiped and prayed to the Moon goddess, waving branches at the new moon – and elephants have been symbols of piety ever since.

• Some early stamps of India were watermarked with an elephant's head; elephants have also appeared on the flag of Siam and Sierra Leone 10-dollar coins.

• Elephants have long been popular characters in children's stories. Rudyard Kipling described how the elephant got his trunk in his charming tale called *The Elephant's Child* in the *Just So Stories*. He also created *Hathi* who heads the elephant patrol in *The Jungle Book*. Other popular elephant characters include those featured in books by more recent authors such as *Babar the Elephant* who first appeared in the 1930s in the books of Jean de Brunhoff and *Elmer: the Story of a Patchwork Elephant* by David McKee.

• Elephant characters have appeared in many films, such as the animated classic, *Dumbo*, released in 1941, and several elephant performers have featured in the many *Tarzan* movies, which first started to appear in the earliest silent-movie days.

• The elephant has inspired artists from the earliest times, with images created on cave walls in primitive Stone Age portrayals leading on to fascinating rock carvings created in many parts of the world throughout the centuries.

• Paintings done by elephants have been exhibited in galleries worldwide and even sold at Christie's auction house for thousands of pounds.

• September 22nd is Elephant Appreciation Day.

Index